The Abortion Debate

Series Editor: Cara Acred

Volume 231

673460

Independence Educational Publishers

First published by Independence Educational Publishers

The Studio, High Green

Great Shelford

Cambridge CB22 5EG

England

© Independence 2012

Photocopy licence

The material in this book is protected by copyright. However, the
purchaser is free to make multiple copies of particular articles for instructional
purposes for immediate use within the purchasing institution.
Making copies of the entire book is not permitted.

British Library Cataloguing in Publication Data

The abortion debate. – (Issues ; v. 231)

1. Abortion – Moral and ethical aspects. 2. Abortion.

I. Series II. Acred, Cara.

363.4'6-dc23

ISBN-13: 9781 86168 624 4

Printed in Great Britain

MWL Print Group Ltd

Contents

Introduction

The Abortion Debate is Volume 231 in the *Issues* series. The aim of the series is to offer current, diverse information about important issues in our world, from a UK perspective.

ABOUT THE ABORTION DEBATE

Abortion describes the medical procedure for the premature termination of pregnancy. A continuously controversial topic, the issues surrounding abortion are examined again and again in political, medical and ethical debates. With extreme views in both pro-life and pro-choice camps and a growing number of people occupying a middle ground between the two, this is a topic that should be thoroughly and sensitively explored. This book offers medical facts alongside many different opinions and explores the legal and ethical debates surrounding abortion.

OUR SOURCES

Titles in the *Issues* series are designed to function as educational resource books, providing a balanced overview of a specific subject.

The information in our books is comprised of facts, articles and opinions from many different sources, including:

- Newspaper reports and opinion pieces

- Website fact sheets

- Magazine and journal articles

- Statistics and surveys

- Government reports

- Literature from special interest groups

A NOTE ON CRITICAL EVALUATION

Because the information reprinted here is from a number of different sources, readers should bear in mind the origin of the text and whether the source is likely to have a particular bias when presenting information (or when conducting their research). It is hoped that, as you read about the many aspects of the issues explored in this book, you will critically evaluate the information presented.

It is important that you decide whether you are being presented with facts or opinions. Does the writer give a biased or unbiased report? If an opinion is being expressed, do you agree with the writer? Is there potential bias to the 'facts' or statistics behind an article?

ASSIGNMENTS

In the back of this book, you will find a selection of assignments designed to help you engage with the articles you have been reading and to explore your own opinions. Some tasks will take longer than others and there is a mixture of design, writing and research based activities that you can complete alone or in a group.

FURTHER RESEARCH

At the end of each article we have listed its source and a website that you can visit if you would like to conduct your own research. Please remember to critically evaluate any sources that you consult and consider whether the information you are viewing is accurate and unbiased.

Abortion

Information from politics.co.uk.

What is abortion?

Abortion describes the medical procedure for the premature termination of pregnancy.

Abortion procedures change according to the gestation (stage) of the pregnancy. The gestation is measured in weeks counting from the first day of the woman's last menstrual period. These methods range from the administration of drugs at early stages, through to 'vacuum aspiration' and medical induction at the latter stages of the pregnancy.

Abortion is legal in Great Britain, but not in Northern Ireland. However, it must be carried out in an authorised environment (usually an NHS hospital), and only after the certification of two registered medical practitioners, except in certain emergencies.

Background

The legal status of abortion has shifted considerably with social values. In the 18th century, English common law allowed abortion, provided it was carried out before the mother felt the foetus move ('quickening').

The Offences Against the Person Act of 1861 made abortion a criminal offence punishable by imprisonment from three years to life. This was reversed by the Infant Life Preservation Act of 1929, which amended the law so that abortion would no longer be regarded as a criminal offence if it were proven to be carried out in 'good faith for the sole purpose of preserving the life of the mother'.

The Abortion Act 1967 (as amended) regulates the modern process of abortion. The Act provides a number of criteria to be fulfilled before a pregnancy can be terminated, although opponents argue the procedure is too simple.

In 2003, the Department of Health produced a Strategy Implementation Action Plan, identifying regional differences in service provision as a major problem.

Controversies

There is much controversy surrounding abortion. The debate may be simplified by dividing it into the opinions of those who support women's rights to abortion, who are called 'pro-choice', and those who oppose it, who are called 'pro-life'.

'Pro-choice' proponents centre their concerns on the rights of the woman. They argue that moves to abolish the right of pregnant mothers to opt for abortion are paternalistic and deny women control over their own bodies. They argue further that abortion is a permanent feature of society, thus the practical result of a ban would merely be to remove clinical guidelines from abortion and push it underground, placing women at serious risk.

'Pro-life' proponents focus the debate on the rights of the unborn child. To a greater or lesser degree, the pro-life party believes that life – as protected by the right to life – begins at conception.

In other countries, the debate is far more intense than in the UK: in the US, doctors prepared to carry out abortions have been attacked and even murdered by pro-life campaigners.

Between the positions at either end of the spectrum, there is a range of ethical, political and medical debate about how easy access to abortion should be, which interests and factors should prevail over others, and how late terminations may be carried out.

> **'The legal status of abortion has shifted considerably with social values'**

In recent years the issue of viability has been pushed to the forefront of debate. Advances in ultrasound technology have produced highly detailed images of foetuses in gestation. Most scientists argue we know nothing new or compelling about the development of foetuses, and therefore have no objective grounds to reducing the abortion time limit. However, the pictures provide an emotional argument for the rights of the foetus, appearing to show foetuses smiling or 'walking' in the womb.

Recent developments

By 2007 it appeared a concerted attempt was underway to recede abortion rights in the UK. A succession of Private Members' Bills went before parliament but were rejected by MPs. Nadine Dorries had attempted to reduce the abortion time limit from 24 to 21 weeks. Pro-abortion campaigners argued late abortion is a rare procedure in the UK – and one often sought by women from overseas who have been forced to travel for treatment.

Ann Winterton put forward a Bill to introduce a mandatory seven-day 'cooling off' period for any woman seeking an abortion. This was defeated by MPs, as was a Private Members' Bill by Angela Watkinson, who said women under 16 should receive 'parental guidance' before having an abortion.

At the other end of the scale, there was mounting pressure from doctors to liberalise abortion access in the early stages of pregnancy. British legislation does not allow for abortion on demand but requires the consent of two doctors. In 2007 the British Medical Association voted it should be treated as any other medical treatments and offered on the basis of the patient's informed consent.

In autumn 2007 a review of the Abortion Act 1967 by the Commons' Science and Technology Committee re-opened the debate. MPs recommended dropping the requirement for two doctors' signatures, dismissing the precaution in safety terms.

The Government agreed, stating: 'We were not presented with any good evidence that, at least in the first trimester, the requirement for two doctors' signatures serves to safeguard women or doctors in any meaningful way, or serves any other useful purpose.' The Government was also concerned that the requirement for two signatures 'may be causing delays in access to abortion services'.

The following year amendments were tabled during the final Commons debate on the Human Fertilisation and Embryology Bill, which would have allowed one doctor to sanction an abortion, thereby ending the two signature rule. The amendments would also have allowed nurses to perform abortions and would have legalised abortions in Northern Ireland.

Initially MPs were to be allowed a free vote on the amendments. However, at the last minute, Gordon Brown instructed Leader of the Commons, Harriet Harman, to put forward a motion which effectively prevented the amendments from being voted upon and so the changes were not introduced. An earlier amendment to the Bill, supported by Conservative leader David Cameron, which would have reduced the 24 week abortion time limit was also defeated by the Government.

But the debate continues with the pro-choice groups still calling for the changes sought by the 2008 amendments and the pro-life groups still seeking a reduction in the abortion time limit. In an interview with the *Catholic Herald* in April 2010, David Cameron said he believed a review of the time limit was needed, suggesting that 'an upper limit of 20 or 22 weeks would be sensible'. However, he also stressed he felt it was 'an issue of conscience' and that a free vote should be allowed on this issue.

Quotes

'If a woman feels that an abortion is in her or her family's best interests, then she should have access to safe, supportive and non-judgemental advice and help from an expert clinic. No one else should pressure her into either continuing with the pregnancy or having an abortion.'

Marie Stopes International – 2010

'No-one has the right to destroy the life of any innocent human being from fertilisation to natural death.'

Oxford University Pro-Life Society – 2010

⇨ Information from politics.co.uk. Please visit www.politics.co.uk for more information.

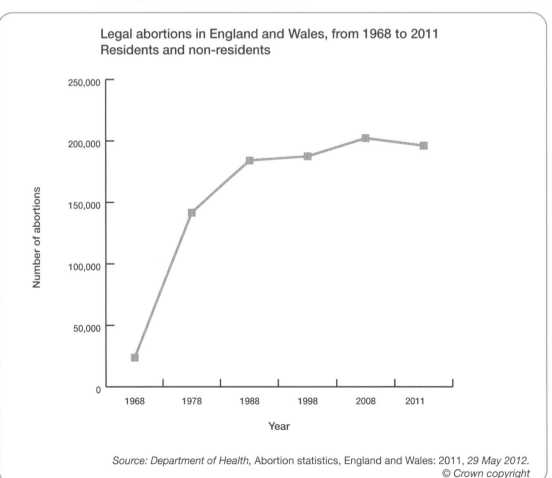

Legal abortions in England and Wales, from 1968 to 2011
Residents and non-residents

Source: Department of Health, Abortion statistics, England and Wales: 2011, *29 May 2012.*
© Crown copyright

Abortion laws

There are different laws for abortion in England, Wales and Scotland, in Northern Ireland and in Jersey. Please make sure you are looking at the right information.

England, Wales and Scotland

In England, Wales and Scotland abortion is legal if you are less than 24 weeks pregnant and if two doctors agree that it is necessary for one of the following reasons:

⇨ having a baby would upset your mental or physical health more than having an abortion. This means you need to explain how you feel the pregnancy would affect your life to a doctor;

⇨ having the baby would harm the mental or physical health of any children you already have.

An abortion is also legal at any time in pregnancy if two doctors agree that:

⇨ an abortion is necessary to save your life

⇨ an abortion would prevent serious permanent harm to your mental or physical health

⇨ there is a high risk that the baby would be seriously handicapped.

The number of weeks pregnant you are is calculated from the first day of your last period. It doesn't matter if you don't know exactly, a doctor will help you work it out.

Northern Ireland

Unfortunately, abortion is not legal in Northern Ireland. The only legal reason for a woman being allowed an abortion in Northern Ireland is when there is a serious risk to her mental or physical health and the risk is permanent or long term.

This means that women in Northern Ireland cannot arrange to have an abortion there. However, there is the option of travelling to England, Scotland or Wales and arranging an abortion there. This does mean that women from Northern Ireland aren't entitled to NHS treatment and have to pay to have an abortion at a private clinic.

If you are in Northern Ireland and need more information on travelling for an abortion, you will need to contact a private abortion service like Marie Stopes on 0845 300 80 90 or BPAS on 08457 30 40 30.

You can get confidential advice and counselling from the FPA in Northern Ireland by calling 0845 122 8687 or, if you are under 19, from the Brook Centre in Belfast.

Jersey

In Jersey it is legal to have an abortion if two doctors agree that one of the following applies:

⇨ the woman is no more than 12 weeks pregnant and it is causing her distress;

⇨ the woman is no more than 24 weeks pregnant and the baby is suffering from a severe incurable abnormality which would cause it to be born with the expectation of an exceedingly poor quality of life;

⇨ an abortion is necessary to save the woman's life or to prevent grave permanent injury to her physical or mental health.

If you need more information on abortion, contact Ask Brook on 0808 802 1234. Your call will be confidential. That means we won't tell anyone about it.

⇨ The above information is reprinted with kind permission from Brook. Please visit www.brook.org.uk for further information on this and other subjects.

© Brook

Abortion: the full story

Information from Mental Healthy.

By Charlotte Fantelli

Abortion: a subject so taboo and controversial that it is only spoken about in a whispered hush, the only loud voices seeming to come from those with agendas of their own.

Many activists put political, religious and moral debate of higher importance than the real and disturbing facts of the situation. Lives of mothers, fathers and children are being hurt by lack of information, counselling and support, before, during and after an unexpected pregnancy (whatever choice one makes).

One in three

With one in three women admitting to having an abortion by the age of 45, we believe it is about time that the whole picture of abortion was discussed. Mental Healthy has teamed up with CareConfidential, a charity which provides unbiased pregnancy and abortion counselling, to bring you a complete picture of the choices available to those who find themselves facing an unplanned pregnancy, and the physical and psychological repercussions of those options. This feature was originally published in *Uncovered Magazine* issue 3.

'No woman wants an abortion. Either she wants a child or she wishes to avoid pregnancy'

The debate

When it comes to this topic, emotions run very high, whatever side of the fence you sit, whether it is pro-choice or pro-life (although these terms seem very much overused and little-understood!)

There seem to be inflamed, impassioned arguments sprouting up all over the place (just look at Twitter to find some disturbing conversations), with little factual or beneficial information being given.

We are not here to argue, to moralise or demoralise; we are here to discuss, to educate and to understand. After all, at Mental Healthy we are passionate about education and better understanding – without these there is no informed choice at all.

What is elective abortion?

Women may face the decision to terminate a pregnancy for many reasons; a small percentage will consider this for medical reasons, or perhaps because of a rape or abuse. Most who opt for an abortion do so due to personal circumstances, this is called an 'elective' abortion and is what we mainly discuss in this feature.

'Women may face the decision to terminate a pregnancy for many reasons'

Abortion figures

We live in a country where access to contraception is incredible and in most instances free. However, even with increased access to family planning services, contraception and information, abortion had steadily risen over the last decade.

There were 189,100 abortions in England and Wales in 2009 – that is the equivalent of 518 abortions

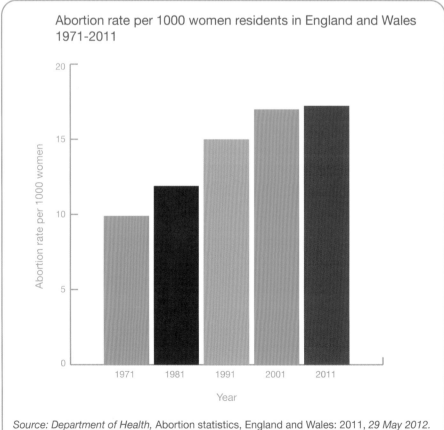

Abortion rate per 1000 women residents in England and Wales 1971-2011

Source: Department of Health, Abortion statistics, England and Wales: 2011, *29 May 2012.*
© Crown copyright

being performed every day, so we have to ask ourselves: why?

'Lives of mothers, fathers and children are being hurt by lack of information, counselling and support'

Is it, as the pro-choice activists would have us believe, because as it becomes less and less stigmatised women are exercising their right to have this procedure? Or is it, as the pro-lifers would have us believe, that the value put on life is slipping, and, as access grows, moral standards decline and it becomes more socially acceptable, with more and more pregnancies terminated?

In reality, I expect both could be considered true reasons for the increase. Finding yourself facing an unplanned pregnancy is scary, and the quicker you can get help and support the better.

Medical advances and English law make it very easy for a woman to have a 'quick' abortion. However, abortion is rarely an easy choice to make, and the 'quick' availability can leave little time for proper counselling.

'There needs to be better sex education before pregnancy, and better counselling for those considering an abortion'

The women behind the numbers

Many women are given numbers and sent to clinics, and while this suits some women whose minds are made up and whose decisions are their own, others are suffering as we lose the human stories behind these numbers. So what is going wrong in our culture that means so many women find themselves in this position?

Perhaps we live in such a privileged culture that our self-satisfying actions rarely have the consequences they once did? Perhaps we should all be happy we live in the 'live now, fix it later' era that is the 21st century – who doesn't enjoy parties, sex and a bit of excess? But the scary thing is that mental health problems have never been so widespread; depression, crime and drug abuse all keep rising, so does this show a society happy with its actions?

Of those who do have an abortion, a significant number suffer emotional, psychological and mental health issues afterwards.

Even if a woman doesn't regret terminating a pregnancy, I'd expect nearly all women have some regret at putting themselves in the position of having to make that choice. A great quote to this effect is: 'No woman wants an abortion. Either she wants a child or she wishes to avoid pregnancy.' Of course it is not always that black and white.

I am one of those one in three women 'behind the numbers'. Researching and writing this article has been extremely hard for me, as it was the biggest regret of my life, and one of the reasons why my mental health suffered, which in turn led to the creation of *Uncovered Magazine* and in turn Mental Healthy.

I am not here to preach, far from it; my personal experience is just that, one experience, and what I went through does not give me the right to decide anyone else's fate, but what it does give me is knowledge of the complete lack of support that was offered to me when I was faced with a very scary situation.

This is why in writing this I have fought long and hard to bring facts and balance, searched many websites, books and organisations to find out how we can, as a society, better equip people to avoid finding themselves in this situation.

Education

While abortion gives many mothers and fathers a way out, it is far better to practise safe sex until a time you choose to become parents. We often associate unplanned pregnancy with the young and we can be quick to blame poor sex education.

'Abortions among older women are consistently high'

A sobering fact to consider is that abortions among older women are consistently high, with more abortions taking place in those over 30 than in those under 20. This goes to prove that it doesn't matter how old you are, you're never to old to learn more about available contraception.

'When it comes to this topic, emotions run very high, whatever side of the fence you sit'

The only healthy way to protect body and mind is to be informed from a young age that sex can be wonderful, enjoyable and most of all safe.

Pregnancy too can be a fantastic blessing, if and when it is wanted. Your contraceptive choices need to be made, and your own views evaluated, before you find yourself with your back very much up against the wall.

We believe that there needs to be better contraceptive and sex education before pregnancy, and better counselling and support for those considering an abortion.

Crisis pregnancy help

Visit: www.careconfidential.com or call the CareConfidential Helpline for impartial and confidential advice: 0800 028 2228.

⇨ The above information is reprinted with kind permission from Charlotte Fantelli. Please visit www.mentalhealthy.co.uk for further information.

© Charlotte Fantelli

Abortion: what happens

If you've decided to have an abortion, here's what you can expect.

If your GP or a doctor at a community contraceptive clinic confirms that you're pregnant, and you've decided to have an abortion, you'll be referred to the clinic or hospital where the abortion will take place, and you'll be assessed.

Your assessment

The assessment will be the same if you go directly to an independent provider (such as BPAS or Marie Stopes) without going to your GP.

During the assessment you:

⇨ can talk to a doctor about the abortion method that will be used

⇨ can ask any questions that you may have

⇨ might be tested for sexually transmitted infections (STI's) and anaemia (low iron levels)

⇨ might be given an ultrasound scan if there's doubt about how many weeks pregnant you are.

BPAS (the British Pregnancy Advisory Service) has produced videos explaining what to expect when you visit a BPAS clinic. The information may also be useful if you are considering an abortion at a clinic that is not BPAS. The videos talk about the consultation, medical abortion and surgical abortion under local or general anaesthetic.

Will I have to stay in hospital?

It depends how many weeks pregnant you are and which abortion method is being used. Normally, you can go home the same day. If it's a late abortion (between 20–24 weeks), you'll usually have to stay overnight.

What happens exactly?

Medical abortion

Medical abortions are used from nine to 20 weeks of pregnancy. The first drug that you take, called mifepristone, blocks the production of hormones that enable the pregnancy to continue. A couple of days later, you have a second appointment where you take another drug called prostaglandin, which causes the lining of the uterus (womb) to break down. This causes bleeding about four to six hours later. You may have to stay at the clinic while this happens.

Surgical abortion

There are two methods. Suction aspiration involves inserting a tube into the uterus through the vagina and removing the pregnancy using suction. It's usually carried out under local anaesthetic, which is injected into the cervix. Most women go home a few hours later.

Dilation and evacuation is used after 15 weeks. The cervix is gently stretched and dilated to enable special forceps and suction to remove the pregnancy.

It usually takes between ten and 20 minutes to perform under general anaesthetic (that means you'll be asleep while it happens). If there are no complications, you can usually go home that same day.

Does having an abortion hurt?

You'll have some period-type pain or discomfort. The later the abortion, the more painful it may be. You'll be advised about taking appropriate painkillers.

With suction abortions, the injection to numb the cervix can sometimes be painful. The procedure itself can be a little uncomfortable, says Dr Tom Coffey, a GP in Wandsworth. 'It's a bit like having a five-minute cervical smear,' he explains.

After any type of abortion, you could also experience some bleeding for up to 14 days afterwards, and period-type pains.

How late into the pregnancy can I have an abortion?

Abortion is legal in Great Britain at any time up to 24 weeks of pregnancy. Most abortions are carried out in the first 14 weeks, and are safer and easier the earlier they are carried out, so it's important to seek advice sooner rather than later.

There are some exceptions. If the mother's life is at risk, or if the child would be born with a severe physical or mental disability, an abortion may be carried out after 24 weeks.

What are my options?

It largely depends on how far into the pregnancy you are. A doctor can talk you through the different methods available.

How long will I have to wait?

Waiting times vary around the country but, as a rule, you shouldn't have to wait for more than three weeks from your initial appointment to having an abortion.

Can I be refused an abortion?

It's rare for anyone to be refused an abortion. A doctor may have moral objections to abortion, but if that's the case they should refer you to another doctor who can help. It can be very difficult to get later abortions, so the earlier you seek help the better.

By law, two doctors have to agree that you can have an abortion. Usually this is the first doctor you see and a second doctor who will perform the abortion, or one who works at the community contraceptive clinic or hospital.

Will it be confidential?

Yes, all information is kept confidential and nobody else will know about it, not even your partner or parents. You can also ask the hospital or clinic not to inform your GP.

If you are under 16, your doctor does not have to mention it to your parents. He or she will encourage you to involve your parents or another supportive adult, but you don't have to so long as the doctor believes that you're competent and can make the decision yourself.

You can ask to have the abortion somewhere other than your local hospital if you wish.

Can I get any counselling before or afterwards?

Most abortion services offer counselling if you feel you need help with any worries or feelings you're having. It's normal to experience a range of emotions after an abortion, such as relief, sadness, happiness or feelings of loss. Each woman's response is unique. To find out what support is available in your area, ask your GP or family planning doctor.

Are there any risks?

There's a risk of infection afterwards, so you may be given antibiotics. In rare cases, the uterus may perforate.

⇨ Damage to the uterus happens in less than one in 1,000 medical abortions performed between 12 and 24 weeks, and up to four in 1,000 surgical abortions.

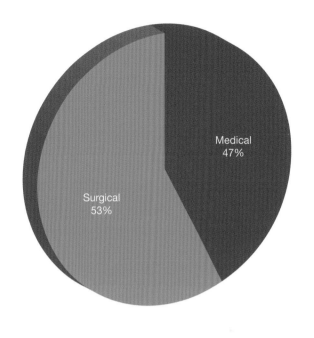

Percentage of medical and surgical legal abortions, 2011
Out of a total 189,931

Medical 47%

Surgical 53%

Source: Department of Health, Abortion statistics, England and Wales: 2011, 29 May 2012.
© Crown copyright

⇨ Damage to the cervix happens in no more than ten in every 1,000 abortions.

⇨ One in 1,000 women who have an abortion will suffer a haemorrhage (excessive bleeding).

Go back to your doctor or clinic straight away if you get symptoms of an infection after an abortion, including:

⇨ high temperature,

⇨ vaginal discharge, or

⇨ abdominal pain that doesn't improve after taking painkillers.

There's a small chance that you'll need further treatment because the abortion hasn't worked. "If you have signs of still being pregnant afterwards, have another pregnancy test," says Dr Coffey. 'If it's positive, you'll have a scan to confirm that the termination hasn't worked, and you'll have the procedure again.'

Will it affect my ability to have a baby in the future?

'Not unless you have recurrent late terminations,' says Dr Coffey. The Royal College of Obstetricians and Gynaecologists (RCOG) states that if there are no problems with your abortion it won't affect your chances of becoming pregnant, although you may have a slightly higher risk of miscarriage or early birth.

Research has shown no definite link between a previous abortion and early labour.

Could I get pregnant again immediately afterwards?

Yes. 'Some women can get pregnant within four weeks of having a termination,' says Dr Coffey. 'So make sure you start using contraception immediately afterwards if you want to avoid getting pregnant again.'

⇨ Reprinted with kind permission of the Department of Health. Please visit www.nhs.uk for further information on this and other subjects.

© Department of Health 2011

Alternatives to abortion

Information from UK Health Centre.

Continuing with the pregnancy

For many women there is no doubt in their minds that they must carry on with the pregnancy and for some they are convinced that they will bring the child up themselves. It may be that family and friends have offered their support and this confirms that you feel you will be able to cope. However, continuing with your pregnancy doesn't mean you have to be a mum once the baby is born though. There are other options available to you and your baby when it arrives.

'Adoption means that your baby will live and be brought up forever by 'new' parents'

Fostering or adoption

One option available to you after giving birth to your baby is adoption or fostering. This means that you do not end your pregnancy but once the baby arrives you will give it up for adoption or fostering.

Adoption means that your baby will live and be brought up forever by 'new' parents and you will have no say in how or where your baby is brought up. You will not be able to contact your baby one they have been adopted. Adoption is a legal process and you will cut all legal ties with your child.

Fostering is less permanent and it means that your baby will be placed with a foster carer who will bring up your child alongside you and your local authority. It has no legal contract like adoption does. It may mean that in the future you may be able to take over the caring responsibilities of your child yourself and become a family.

For more information on fostering and adoption you can either contact your local social services department or the British Association of Adoption and Fostering or Adoption UK Charity.

'Everyone is different and what is the right decision for one woman may not be the right one for you'

Having a termination or abortion

Continuing with your pregnancy may not be an option for you. You might just feel too scared to even think about having the baby so continuing with your pregnancy may not be an option for you. Everyone is different and what is the right decision for one woman may not be the right one for you. This is where the role of all the support, advice and guidance comes in from the professional counsellors at specialist clinics. These specially trained counsellors will support you through the decisions you will have to make and explain to you all the options and the pros and cons, of each. They will discuss the different abortion options you can have and what will happen during the procedure.

'You might just feel too scared to even think about having the baby'

The types of abortion procedure you may have depends on how many weeks pregnant you are and if you want to be awake or asleep. If you have any medical conditions, this may also affect which types of abortions you can have.

⇨ The above information is reprinted with kind permission from UK Health Centre. Please visit www.healthcentre.org.uk for further information on this and other subjects.

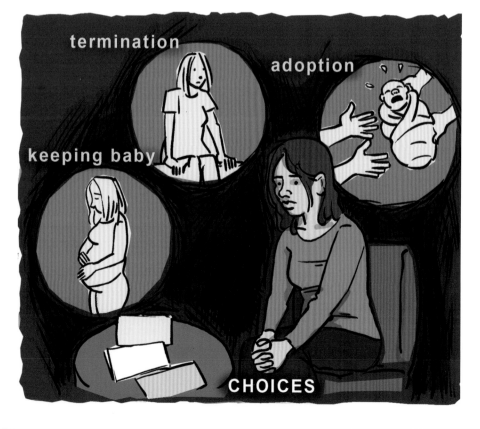

© UK Health Centre 2012

Men and abortion

Information from Lighthouse Family Trust.

Talking with your partner

Men and women communicate in very different ways. Women place a lot of emphasis on first impressions and in this situation even a neutral reaction may be seen as a lack of support. One woman said she had an abortion because her partner's first reaction was 'Okay, I don't mind either way.' Another because her partner casually said 'If you want' and changed the subject. Both women took this casualness to be a lack of interest and support, but found out later that all their partners needed was time to adjust to the new situation. If you really want to help your partner you should talk openly and frankly, get as much information as possible and don't base your decision on the results of one conversation. Above all ask your partner to give you time to think things through.

'It was only years later I realised that I had never settled down and got married because of the abortion'

You may feel that, because of the way society has labelled abortion as a 'woman's issue', your partners decision has nothing to do with you. You may think that your partner should be taking this decision on her own. But is this true?

With many couples the responsibility for an abortion decision also rests with the man because few women will have an abortion against the wishes of a supportive partner. Her response will depend on how you react. What your partner needs to know is what you truly think. Saying 'whatever you want' still leaves the weight on her shoulders.

Your partner needs reassurance that you are not planning to abandon her. That you care enough to face with her the consequences of your sexual relationship.

Effects of abortion

Generally men know very little about abortion. Abortion is not something to be considered lightly – there are physical and mental health risks to abortion.

Trauma from an abortion can also affect men. Guilt and hurt after an abortion can drive couples apart, especially if one partner was unsure about the decision. Often couples split up following an abortion.

You may want your relationship back to where it used to be, but this is impossible. Sometimes men react with a gut instinct that it is better to do something quickly and worry about the consequences later. A common reaction is 'get rid of it'. But this is not one of those situations, and an abortion will not put things back as they were. In short, both you and your partner have been permanently changed by the pregnancy.

Some men feel guilty about what they have done and then find it difficult to form close relationships in the future. Some disguise their feelings by remaining emotionally cold and distant. One man said 'following the abortion I split up with my girlfriend and it was only years later I realised that I had never settled down and got married because of the abortion'.

There is a deep instinct in men to protect women and children. An abortion can undermine a man's confidence in himself and he can come to think of himself as a failure – a failure as a partner, a failure as a father, a failure as a man.

Many men's lives have been harmed by abortion. That is why it is important that you are involved in the decision, allow yourself plenty of time to think things through and talk openly with your partner.

Making your decision

If you really want to help your partner be honest with her. This is a tough and confusing situation. But it can also be a chance to change and mature. Are you going to run? Or will you take the first steps of genuine love by staying with her when the going gets tough? In either case, your partner is not the only one who has to make some important choices.

⇨ The above information is reprinted with kind permission from Lighthouse Family Trust. Please visit www.lighthouseft. org.uk for further information on this and other subjects.

© 2011 Lighthouse Family Trust

What the statistics tell us

Commentary on the Department of Health's 2012 abortion statistics.

Where do abortion statistics come from?

Each year, the Department of Health (DH) collects statistics for abortions carried out in England and Wales. The statistics are taken from the abortion notification forms (HSA4), which all doctors are legally obliged to fill out. Official statistics have been gathered since 1968, when abortion was first legally available in England and Wales.

Abortion is not legal in Northern Ireland, except in very exceptional circumstances.

The DH statistics include all abortions that take place in England and Wales, and separates the figures on abortions to women resident in England and Wales.

What the statistics can tell us

The national abortion statistics provide a useful and accurate way of assessing how many legal abortions are carried out in England and Wales in any given year, and how these statistics have changed since 1968. They can also tell us the legal grounds under which abortions were carried out under the 1967 Abortion Act. However, numbers never tell the whole story, and care should be taken in interpreting the stats.

What the statistics cannot tell us

The national statistics cannot tell us the reasons why women have abortions: they can only tell us the grounds under which doctors decided that an abortion was legal. Nor can they tell us the extent of illegal abortion. We do not know how many abortions took place before 1968, for example. Nor do we know how many abortions take place illegally today – for example, by women using drugs bought off the Internet.

However, given the steady rise in official numbers of legal abortions since 1968, and the improvements in access to abortion (discussed in the following sections), we can assume that the vast majority of abortions carried out in England and Wales today are legal ones, and that the national statistics provide us with an accurate picture.

Some abortion statistics – often those that catch media attention – need to be treated with particular caution, and these are examined below. These include repeat abortions, and teenage pregnancy and abortion rates.

How many abortions are there?

In 2011, there were 189,931 abortions to women resident in England and Wales. This is roughly the same (a rise of 0.2%) from 2010. The highest recorded number of abortions to women resident in England and Wales was in 2007, with a total of 198,499.

The total number of abortions carried out in every given year includes non-residents: that is, women who come to England and Wales from abroad. The number of abortions is presented in Table 1 of the official statistics. The figures below give a snapshot of the number of abortions to residents of England and Wales over the past four decades.

⇨ 1969: 49,829

⇨ 1979: 120,611

⇨ 1989: 170,463

⇨ 1999: 173,701

⇨ (2007: 198,499)

⇨ 2011: 189,931

The extent of abortion can best be summed up by the observation, by the Royal College of Obstetricians and Gynaecologists, that 'at least one third of British women will have had an abortion by the time they reach the age of 45 years'.

What is the abortion rate?

The number of abortions in England and Wales reflects the changing size of the population, in that if the population grows, the number of abortions will grow. This means that there are more women having abortions, not necessarily that women are having more abortions. The age-standardised abortion rate, calculated per 1,000 women residents aged 15–44, is a more accurate measure of the extent of abortion than the numbers alone.

In 2011, the age-standardised abortion rate was 17.5 per 1,000

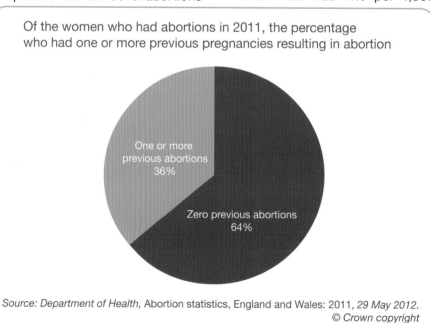

Of the women who had abortions in 2011, the percentage who had one or more previous pregnancies resulting in abortion

One or more previous abortions 36%

Zero previous abortions 64%

Source: Department of Health, Abortion statistics, England and Wales: 2011, *29 May 2012.*
© Crown copyright

women residents aged 15–44, the same as in 2009 and 2010. This means that of every 1,000 women of reproductive age living in England and Wales, seventeen and a half of them can be expected to have an abortion.

The abortion rate began to be calculated in 1969, and has generally risen since then. As with the number of abortions, the highest recorded rate to date was in 2007, of 18.6 per 1,000 women residents aged 15–44. The abortion rate has fallen over the four years since then.

⇨ 1969: 5.2 per 1,000 women

⇨ 1979: 11.5 per 1,000 women

⇨ 1989: 15.1 per 1,000 women

⇨ 1999: 16.8 per 1,000 women

⇨ (2007: 18.6 per 1,000 women)

⇨ 2011: 17.5 per 1,000 women

What is the birth rate?

In 2010 the Total Fertility Rate (TFR) for England and Wales increased to 2.00 children per woman from 1.96 in 2009. There were 723,165 live births, compared with 706,248 in 2009 (a rise of 2.4%).

(Office for National Statistics, Statistical Bulletin: Births and Deaths in England and Wales, 2010. 13 July 2011)

Figures from the Office for National Statistics show that there were an estimated 909,245 conceptions in England and Wales in 2010, compared with 896,466 in 2009, an increase of 1.4%. Conception rates in 2010 increased in all age groups, with the exception of women aged under 20. The under-18 conception rate for 2010 is the lowest since 1969, at 35.5 conceptions per 1,000 women aged 15–17. The estimated number of conceptions to women aged under 18 also fell to 34,633 in 2010, compared with 38,259 in 2009, a decline of 9.5%; the estimated number of conceptions to girls aged under 16 was 6,674 in 2010, compared with 7,158 in 2009 (a decrease of 6.8%).

The percentage of conceptions leading to a legal abortion varies by age group. Over the past decade, this proportion has generally

increased for women aged under 20, remained stable for women in their twenties and early thirties, and decreased for women aged 35 and over. In 2010, about 60% of conceptions to women under 16 ended in abortion, as did about 12% of conceptions to women aged 30–34. The most striking decline is in the percentage of conceptions leading to abortion for women aged 40 and over – down from about 43% in 1990 to 29% in 2010.

(Office for National Statistics, Statistical Bulletin: Conceptions in England and Wales 2010. 28 February 2012.)

How many women come to Britain from overseas to have an abortion?

In 2011, there were 189,931 abortions carried out to residents of England and Wales, and 6,151 to non-residents. 'Non-residents' means women who come to England and Wales for abortions because the procedure is illegal in their own country: in 2011, they principally came from Northern Ireland (16%) and the Irish Republic (67%). Non-resident women do not receive abortion treatment on the NHS.

The number of abortions to non-residents in 2011 is the lowest recorded since 1969. However, these numbers have in fact been falling gradually since 1973, when 56,581 abortions were recorded to non-residents. These numbers should be treated with caution, as they can be affected by the availability of abortion in other European countries, and also by the funding of abortion by the NHS in England and Wales.

How many women have 'repeat' abortions?

Figures on 'repeat abortions' often provoke shocked headlines in the press. But these statistics need to be treated with caution for a number of reasons.

In 2011, one third (36%) of women undergoing abortions had one or more previous abortions. The proportion of 'repeat abortions' has risen from 31% since 2001. One quarter (26%) of abortions to

women aged under 25 in 2011 were 'repeat abortions'.

The phrase 'repeat abortion' implies that women are having serial abortions: this is not the case. The phrase used by the national statistics is 'previous abortion', which is a more accurate and less sensational description of the issue.

The statistics show that 26% who have abortions have had 'one or more' previous abortion. The proportion of women who have had more than one previous abortion is roughly 9%. When one considers that, in England and Wales, there are an estimated two million acts of heterosexual coitus in women per day, it is striking that only one in 1,000 acts of sex result in an abortion. (See 'Is repeat abortion a problem?', by Sam Rowlands. In *Abortion Review Special Edition 2: Abortion and Women's Lives*.)

In modern Britain, women may require more than one abortion because they are exposed to greater risk of unwanted pregnancy than women of previous generations. This is because more women choose not to have children, and those who do choose motherhood tend to delay having children until their late 20s or early 30s. The existence of a longer 'window' between women becoming sexually active and starting their families may mean that women are more exposed to unintended pregnancy.

Abortion has become more widely available, and less stigmatised. This means that women may well be more likely to report having had a previous abortion than they would in the past. Policymakers' interest in the number of previous abortions has also encouraged the assiduous collection of these statistics, and flagged 'repeat abortion' as an issue of media interest. Because statistics on previous abortions are reported voluntarily by the woman undergoing abortion, we should be aware that the 'repeat abortion' statistics reflect an emphasis on reporting as much as they reflect the numbers of procedures taking place.

The fact that '26% of abortions to women under 25 were repeat abortions' is often used to present repeat abortion as a problem of feckless young people. However, it should be borne in mind that the abortion rate is highest (at 30 per 1,000 women) for women aged 20–24, who are at the peak of their fertility and increasingly less likely to be actively considering starting a family. Abortions to women under 25 account for over half of all abortions, so it is not surprising that a significant proportion of previous abortions are accounted for by this age group.

'Some have argued that the recession would force the abortion rate up'

The discussion of 'repeat abortion' tends to focus on teenagers, but as the national statistics note, this is 'a complex issue associated with increased age as it allows longer time for exposure to pregnancy risks'. Simplistic attempts to stigmatise 'repeat' abortion ignore the fact that women who will have more than one abortion are less likely to be teenagers than older women who have had previous abortions when they were younger.

Research on repeat abortion suggests that women who have more than one abortion are no different to those who have one abortion: they are no less likely to use contraception, and are certainly not using abortion as a means of contraception.

What factors affect the abortion rate?

It is widely accepted that no one factor 'causes' women to have abortions. In all societies, women have experienced unwanted pregnancies, and sought to induce abortions using drugs, implements, herbal remedies or methods based on 'old wives' tales'. We can assume that the legalisation of abortion makes the abortion rate rise, simply because women and doctors are able to seek and practise the procedure without fear of criminal prosecution. However, we should not assume that if abortion were illegal, women would not have abortions.

Illegal abortion

Where abortion is illegal, it is impossible to determine the extent of the practice. The only statistics there are to go on are from the complications arising from illegal abortions that damaged women: successful abortions that did not harm women were not recorded.

In the BPAS publication *Pioneers of Change* Peter Diggory, one of the doctors who played a key role in bringing the 1967 Abortion Act into existence, recalls that the hospital in which he worked in 1961 'admitted more than 400 women every year suffering from complications of criminal abortion'. Diggory explains:

'How big a problem was criminal abortion? Accurate statistics will never be available. The medical establishment pretended that the numbers were small though the general practitioners knew that this was untrue because they frequently saw women suffering from its complications. Amongst the general public everybody knew a friend or relative who had resorted either to a backstreet abortion or a legal one and the press carried lurid stories of the perils. Women who actually had abortions were very silent about their experience and often displayed great loyalty towards the abortionist, refusing to disclose names even when seriously ill and questioned by the police.'

Legal abortion

As we can see from the abortion statistics for England and Wales, the number of abortions and the abortion rate has risen steadily from the time when it became legally available, in 1968. However, it should be borne in mind that the statistics gathered since legalisation only show the number of abortions recorded, not those carried out. We can assume that in England and Wales today, most women have legal rather than illegal abortions, and that the statistics therefore represent the number of abortions actually taking place. But in 1969 – the first full year for which statistics were recorded – the official statistics would have sat alongside unrecorded illegal abortions.

Available abortion

The availability of abortion is linked to its legalisation. Legal abortion means that women and doctors are able to seek and practise the procedure without fear of criminal prosecution. However, if there are no doctors prepared to perform abortions, or there are no facilities in which legal abortions can be carried out, women will not be able to have abortions – whatever the law says.

In England and Wales, abortion is widely available. The proportion of abortions funded by the National Health Service (NHS) has risen steadily, and in 2011 96% of abortions were funded by the NHS, compared to 94% in 2009. The availability of abortion in England and Wales has been assisted by the fact that 61% of abortions are carried out in approved independent sector places (such as clinics run by BPAS and Marie Stopes) but publicly paid for, showing a trend towards giving women increasing access to specialist services outside the general NHS.

'The reasons women have abortions are primarily to do with their personal circumstances'

There remain issues to do with recruitment and training of doctors in England and Wales who will carry out abortions, particularly to later gestations. These issues tend to impact upon the availability of abortion in relation to the choice of method available to women seeking abortion, and the availability of later-gestation abortions to women with particular health conditions or fetal anomalies.

Economic environment

There has been some discussion about whether the recent global economic recession would affect the abortion rate. Some have argued that the recession would force the abortion rate up, as couples would not be able to support a child, or more children; others have argued that the abortion rate would be forced down, by women losing their jobs and deciding to have a 'recession baby'.

'Under British law, abortion is a decision that is made by a woman and her doctors'

While both these arguments seem plausible, there is no evidence that broad economic conditions have a particular effect on the abortion rate. Historically, the birth rate has tended to fall in conditions of major recession; but the reasons for this decline are impossible to quantify. We do know that poverty itself does not 'cause' abortion, in that couples with low incomes choose to have children as much as do those with higher incomes. We also know that as societies have developed, and become wealthier, the birth rate has historically tended to fall.

'The discussion of "repeat abortion" is a complex issue'

Britain since the recession has experienced no dramatic changes in either the abortion rate or the birth rate. We should be wary about attempting to draw any conclusions about the relationship between macro-economic conditions and reproductive outcomes.

Personal circumstances

Women, quite rightly, do not have to state a particular reason for why they need an abortion; and the national statistics do not tell us anything about 'why' women have abortions. However, research and experience tell us that the reasons why women have abortions are primarily to do with their personal circumstances. These include:

⇨ They may have fallen pregnant unintentionally, and know that raising a child would be difficult at this point in their lives;

⇨ Their contraception may have failed;

⇨ Their relationship with their partner may have broken down, turning a wanted pregnancy into an unwanted pregnancy;

⇨ Their financial or other life circumstances may have changed;

⇨ Health or other problems with their other children;

⇨ Problems with their own physical or mental health;

⇨ A prenatal diagnosis of fetal anomaly, meaning that if they continued their pregnancy to term the baby might be stillborn or born with a disability.

This is by no means an exhaustive list. There is a wide variety of reasons why women decide that they need an abortion, and these decisions are highly personal ones to make.

Under British law, abortion is a decision that is made by a woman and her doctors. In many other countries, women have the right to abortion 'on request' up to a certain gestation of pregnancy.

These 'woman-centred' laws recognise that it is the woman (not her partner) who will carry the pregnancy and give birth to the child. However, this does not mean that women's decisions about abortion are always made on their own, or that their relationships with partners and other family members are unimportant. Research, and experience gathered from BPAS clients, is that most partners of women seeking abortion are supportive of their decision, and that most women are supported through the procedure by friends and family members.

2 May 2012

⇨ Information from Abortion Review. Please visit www. abortionreview.org for more information.

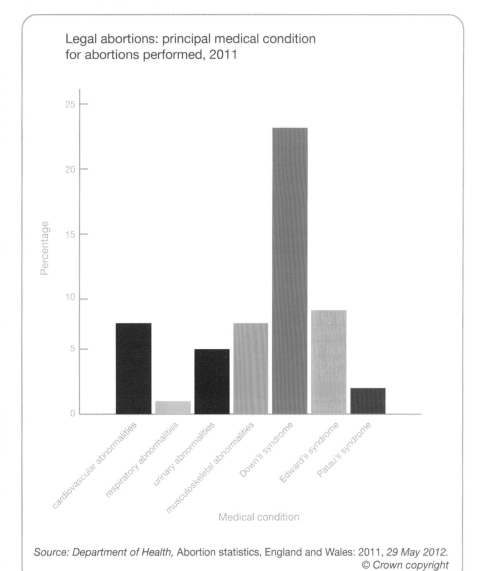

Legal abortions: principal medical condition for abortions performed, 2011

Source: *Department of Health,* Abortion statistics, England and Wales: 2011, *29 May 2012.*
© Crown copyright

Abortion controversy: pro-choice and pro-life

Information from UK Health Centre.

You may have heard lots of information about abortions. Some may have been positive and in favour of them whereas others may have been strongly against them. There is often news of protests going on outside abortion clinics and women feeling intimidated to attend them. Some people believe that you have a right to choose what happens to you while others believe that your foetus or unborn child has the right to life and that should not be taken away from it.

'Pro-choice campaigners aim to ensure that women have the right to choose whether or not to continue with a pregnancy'

The pro-choice abortion argument

Pro-choice campaigners aim to ensure that women have the right to choose whether or not to continue with a pregnancy. They believe that the Abortion Act 1967 should be modernised and that safe, legal abortions should be made readily available to all women as and when they need them.

Your right to choose what you do is imperative to these groups and they feel that the law should be changed to reflect this, removing the need for a doctor to assess you to determine your need for an abortion. They also believe that abortions provided through the NHS can be restrictive and quite often are delayed.

Pro-choice groups are trying to get the current law brought in line with the majority of current public opinion and the mains areas of focus are:

Around three quarters of British people believe that you should be able to make your own decision about having an abortion.

⇨ To remove the need for a doctor to assess you in line with the current laws and approve your abortion request.

⇨ To extend the law to women in Northern Ireland so that they no longer have to travel to access abortion services.

⇨ To reduce NHS waiting times and make the delay between your appointment and abortion no more than three weeks no matter which NHS Trust you go through.

The pro-life abortion argument

Pro-life campaigners aim to protect the right to life from conception, through life to then having a natural death. They believe that all life, including that of a foetus, is precious and should not be ended.

Your pregnancy, your foetus primarily, is important to these groups and they place great significance on the development of it deeming abortion 'unjust and discriminatory'.

While they are completely for your right to choose what you do with your own body and whether or not you have sexual intercourse they are firmly against your right to choose an abortion. There are also groups that do not believe in abortion due to religious beliefs.

'Pro-life campaigners aim to protect the right to life from conception, through life to then having a natural death'

You should try not to be swayed by opinions other than your own and, while this can be difficult, if you find out the information for yourself you can then make an informed decision that is right for you.

'Some people believe that you have a right to choose what happens to you while others believe that your unborn child has the right to life'

⇨ The above information is reprinted with kind permission from UK Health Centre. Please visit www.healthcentre.org.uk for further information on this and other subjects.

© UK Health Centre

Moral and ethical issues

Information from Education for Choice.

Many people have strong views on the morality of abortion. These views may have been formed after a great deal of thought about abortion, or could simply be ideas picked up from friends, family or media. Some people's views on abortion are closely linked to their religious or political beliefs and for others connect more to their personal experiences or even just gut feelings.

People's views on abortion are not necessarily set in stone for life. Like our opinions on many things, we can change our minds as a result of specific incidents, or just adapt with age and experience.

A spectrum of belief

People's views on abortion range from those who believe that abortion is always wrong under any circumstances to those who believe that a woman should always be allowed an abortion for any reason and at any point in pregnancy. Most people's beliefs fall somewhere between these two ends of the spectrum.

Some of the issues here are things people consider when deciding what they think about abortion.

Woman's rights or fetal rights?

Some people believe that the moment of fertilisation marks the beginning of sacred life and that from that moment the zygote/embryo/fetus has an absolute right to life. These people may believe that abortion is always wrong.

Some people believe that a balance must be struck between the rights of the fetus and the rights of the woman and that the rights of the fetus increase as it develops in the womb. These people may believe that abortion is acceptable in some circumstances, for some reasons and/or at some stages of pregnancy.

Others believe that a woman should have an absolute right to decide whether or not to continue with her pregnancy. As it is her body and life that will be affected by pregnancy, childbirth and motherhood, no-one else should have the power to force her to continue with an unwanted pregnancy. Some of these people do not 'like' the idea of abortion and would not choose it themselves, but do believe that women should have the right to choose safe, legal abortion.

Isn't adoption the moral solution?

For some women adoption is a good solution to an unwanted pregnancy. It may be a positive decision to bring a baby into the world, confident that it will be well looked after by adoptive parents; it may be the only morally acceptable option for her; or her pregnancy might have progressed too far to be able to access an abortion.

Most people believe that women should not be coerced or pressured to continue with a pregnancy and have their baby adopted, but that adoption should be positively presented as one of her possible options.

However, some people say that adoption is the only acceptable solution to an unwanted pregnancy and that abortion should not be an option.

'Some people believe that a living person has characteristics that a fetus doesn't'

When does life begin?

Some religions and cultures teach that life begins at fertilisation – the moment that sperm meets egg – and that the fertilised egg is a sacred life, with as many rights as a baby, child or adult.

Medical science tells us that a proportion of fertilised eggs do not become implanted in the woman's womb and that a large proportion of those that do (estimates suggest around 25%) are lost naturally to miscarriage. So some people do not believe that fertilisation is a good point at which to mark the beginning of a sacred life.

'Woman's main role on earth is to conceive, deliver and raise children...'

Other people see the zygote/embryo/fetus as a developing life with rights increasing as pregnancy develops.

Other people believe that the end of pregnancy and birth of a baby marks its transition to personhood and is the point at which it attains rights.

When does a fetus become a person?

This question is important because we do not give human rights (such as the right to life) to all living things (plants, animals, etc.) but only to people. The earliest zygote contains the entire DNA code of the person that could develop from it, and some argue that its potential to become a person is enough to give it the rights of a fully developed person.

Others argue that a person is more than just the sum of its biological parts, and believe that a living person has characteristics that a fetus doesn't. These may include the ability to think and reason or the capacity to respond, to build relationships and to communicate.

Some believe that it is the ability of the fetus to exist independently of the mother that defines it as a person. They consider the fetus to have the right to life at the point where it is 'viable', meaning it can survive outside of the woman's womb.

Is abortion murder?

Some people categorise abortion as murder at even the earliest stages of pregnancy.

Others see this as an emotive term designed to stigmatise both the women who have abortions and doctors who provide abortions.

In the UK, abortion is not legally categorised as murder. When specific criteria are met it is a legal medical procedure.

What about gender abortions?

Sometimes a genetic condition is carried only by the male or female gene so, after identifying the gender of the fetus, parents-to-be might opt for abortion in order to avoid passing on a genetic condition. Some people believe this is an acceptable reason to have an abortion.

Most gender abortions take place because there is a cultural preference for having a baby of a specific gender. In many parts of the world, for example, boy babies are more desirable than girl babies. This is normally a symptom of serious cultural and economic inequality between men and women in those communities. It might relate to the difference in men's and women's access to education, their earning power and status as well as traditions around marriage and dowries which mean that the parents and families of girl children are disadvantaged.

A common reaction people have to gender abortions is that they are very wrong. However, people also recognise that the pressure on a woman to have an abortion because of the gender of the fetus can be enormous. Some unwanted girls are killed after birth, abandoned or seriously mistreated and their mothers punished for their failure to produce boys. Under these circumstances many will not condemn women for having gender abortions.

'Some believe that it is the ability of the fetus to exist independently of the mother that defines it as a person'

Is women's sexuality the real problem?

Although discussion of abortion in the 21st century is largely focused on the issue of fetal rights, there are plenty of people whose objections to abortion are based on a much more traditional concern – the 'problem' of women's sexuality. Often those who condemn abortion on the grounds of the right to life of the fetus also believe that the use of contraception is wrong.

'Woman's main role on earth is to conceive, deliver and raise children'

For some, anxiety about and disapproval of women's sexuality lies at the root of anti-abortion ideas. For them anything that facilitates fornication (sex without the intention or consequence of pregnancy) is morally wrong because the sole purpose of sex is to reproduce. These people believe that contraception and abortion allow women a way to be sexually active without having children, and therefore must be wrong.

Motherhood – the natural way?

Anxiety about abortion and women's sexuality is often connected to the idea that a woman's natural role and destiny is motherhood and that anything disturbing the progression between sex and motherhood is bound to cause a woman psychological problems or mental illness.

This idea was expressed by an American, Doctor Gouldstone, who, in 1958 said: 'Woman's main role on earth is to conceive, deliver and raise children …When this function is interfered with, we see all sorts of emotional disorders.'

Over fifty years later this view of women is still evident in some discussion of abortion. Some people believe that any woman seeking abortion must be unnatural or mentally disturbed or that any woman who has an abortion will become mentally disturbed.

These days many people choose to have small families or not to become parents at all. They do not feel that they are unnatural or disturbed, but are simply people making informed personal choices.

⇨ Information from Education for Choice. Please visit www.efc. org.uk for more information.

© Education for Choice

Religion and abortion

No religion actively supports abortion, but some religions accept that there are situations when abortion may be necessary. A few religions oppose abortion under all circumstances.

Jehovah's Witnesses

The Jehovah's Witnesses and some Evangelical Christian churches teach that abortion is absolutely unacceptable in all circumstances.

Roman Catholic Church

The Roman Catholic Church used to accept abortion up until 'quickening' – the moment at which movement is felt in the womb (normally around 16‒20 weeks). It is only since 1869 that it has taught that sacred life begins at the moment of conception. Abortion is now prohibited under all circumstances and can be punished by exclusion from the church (excommunication).

Orthodox Judaism

Although Orthodox Judaism teaches that life only begins at the moment of birth, abortion is prohibited except where the mother's life is at risk or continuing with the pregnancy will seriously damage her health.

Liberal Judaism, Sikhism, Buddhism

Some religions such as Liberal Judaism and Sikhism teach that a woman and her partner must make the best decision they can taking into account the moral issues involved as well as the practical considerations for a woman's well-being. Buddhism asks

people to search their conscience and make the right decision for themselves.

Hinduism

Hindu scriptures accept abortion only to save a woman's life.

Church of England

The Church of England teaches that abortion is sometimes a 'necessary evil'. There are certain circumstances (for example serious risk to the health of the mother) when her needs override the rights of the fetus. Other Christians such as Methodists teach that personal and social factors need to be considered in each case. Some members of the Methodist church supported the legalisation of abortion in the UK, as they were concerned about the dangers of illegal, unsafe abortion.

Islam

Islam teaches that the actual life of the woman takes precedence over the probable life of the fetus, so abortion is acceptable to prevent harm to the woman's health. Some scholars also sanction abortion if the pregnancy resulted from rape. As it is believed that the fetus becomes 'ensouled' at 120 days, early abortion is considered to be less sinful.

Religion, law and practice

When making decisions about issues such as pregnancy and abortion, people of faith try to balance their real life circumstances with the teachings of their religion. In practice, people of all faiths, in all countries, use abortion as a way to limit family size or space their children where contraception is unavailable or where it has failed to work effectively. In many Latin American countries the strict Catholic prohibition on abortion is reflected in the law and each year women and doctors are imprisoned for having or providing abortions. However, national abortion laws do not always reflect the religion of the country. India, which is a mainly Hindu country, has liberal abortion laws. Many Islamic countries prohibit abortion entirely even for reasons accepted by Islam.

'People of faith try to balance their real life circumstances with the teachings of their religion'

⇨ The above information is reprinted with kind permission from Education for Choice. Please visit www.efc.org.uk for further information.

© Education for Choice

Disability and abortion

Information from Education for Choice.

UK abortion law and disability

The legal limit for most abortions was reduced from 28 weeks to 24 weeks in 1990 because some babies now survive at 24 weeks.

'When there is a substantial risk that if the child were born it would suffer from such physical or mental abnormalities as to be seriously handicapped' there is no legal limit as to when abortion can take place. (Abortion Act 1967)

British abortion law does not specify which disabilities or conditions can or cannot be grounds for abortion after 24 weeks. The decision is left up to the woman and her doctors.

Arguments supporting abortion for disability

The basic argument about abortion for disability reflects current debate about abortion generally. Those who support the right of a woman to opt for abortion because of a diagnosis of fetal abnormality or disability are often supporters of the right to choose in general:

⇨ Women are capable of making informed choices if they have up to date and accurate facts and support from well-trained professionals, educators, friends, partners and families.

⇨ Whatever the reason for the abortion she is probably the best judge of her own circumstances and capacity.

⇨ Women who choose to end pregnancies because of potential disability can be acting out of compassion, knowing that they do not have the ability to care for a child with special needs.

⇨ There is no guarantee that an adoptive family could be found for a seriously disabled child.

⇨ Many people who support women's right to abortion because of potential disability are active supporters of rights for people with disabilities and say that the two positions are completely compatible.

Arguments opposing abortion for disability

Many of those who oppose abortion for disability also oppose the rights of women to choose abortion in general:

⇨ Every fetus is a sacred human life and it is morally wrong to end that life.

⇨ The stage of development of the fetus or its state of health are not relevant as all fetuses should be equally valued.

⇨ It is always better to continue with the pregnancy and put the baby up for adoption than to end the pregnancy.

⇨ Some people who are not opposed to abortion in general are uncomfortable that the law allows for abortion for disability later in pregnancy than for other reasons.

Disability rights perspective

The Disability Rights Commission (DRC) argues that the Abortion Act is 'not inconsistent with the Disability Discrimination Act since the latter is concerned with the rights of living persons. Moreover, the number of terminations made under the [Act] is relatively small, and the DRC has no wish to put in question the Abortion Act as a whole'.

However, the DRC says that the part of the Act concerned with disability 'is offensive to many people; it reinforces negative stereotypes of disability; and there is substantial support for the view that to permit terminations at any point during a pregnancy on the ground of risk of disability, while time limits apply to other grounds set out in the Abortion Act, is incompatible with valuing disability and non-disability equally … the DRC believes the context in which parents choose whether to have a child should be one in which disability and non-disability are valued equally.'

⇨ The above information is reprinted with kind permission from Education for Choice. Please visit www.efc.org.uk for more information.

The abortion time limit and why it should remain at 24 weeks

The obstetricians' and gynaecologists' perspective.

What is the current abortion time limit?

At the moment, it is legal to have an abortion in Great Britain up to the 24th week of gestation.

Why are there calls for the abortion time to be lowered?

Those that want the abortion time limit to be lowered argue that the survival rate of premature babies has improved since 1990, the last time when the law was changed. According to them, medical science and technology have made it easier for premature babies born at 22–24 weeks to survive.

Do premature babies survive earlier now?

No, a large scale study, *EPICure*, was undertaken in 1951 to examine the survival rates of premature babies born in the UK and Ireland at 26 weeks gestation and below. It tracked the progress and health of babies who survived into their tenth month.

'24 weeks appears to be the threshold at which premature babies have a better survival rate'

The results were published in 2000 and showed that the survival rates of babies were better if they are born above 25 weeks. At 24 weeks, the hospital discharge rate was 33.6%. At 23 weeks, this was 19.9% and at 22 weeks, it fell to 9.1%.

It has been widely reported that the *EPICure* 2 study (currently waiting to be published) will show that the survival rate of premature babies has increased at 24 weeks and above but there are insignificant improvements at 23 weeks or below.

Based on the available and anticipated evidence on the neonatal survival rates of premature babies, at the moment, 24 weeks appears to be the threshold at which premature babies have a better survival rate.

Why do babies born below 24 weeks have lower chances of survival?

If born before 26 weeks, many premature babies require very intensive and invasive care, including help with breathing and the removal of waste fluids from their bodies. This is because their lungs and metabolism are not fully developed yet (if they were still in their mother's womb they would be breathing and eating through their mothers). Their skin is also not fully formed and neither are many of the normal bodily functions you would find in a full-term baby. These babies therefore require round-the-clock attention and care in the first few months of their lives.

Recent reports claim that the neonatal survival rates of premature babies in selected hospitals show very promising results and further the case for the time limit being lowered.

The RCOG is delighted whenever good results are recorded. However, with regard to looking at data from one or two neonatal units, and in exclusion to national results, a 'wider' and more accurate picture cannot be derived.

Furthermore, the findings from these studies, though impressive, note that the majority of these premature babies have been transferred to neonatal intensive care units. It is well known that babies that are transferred tend to have a better chance of survival, especially after they have made it through the very precarious first 48 hours of life. If

these babies find themselves in an environment where the prevailing ethos is to resuscitate at whatever costs, then these babies will have a better chance of survival. Likewise, neonatal survival would be better in units that have ready access to a range of specialist care and equipment.

These figures do not represent a true and unbiased picture of the survival rate of premature babies. For this to happen, it is important to look at figures of neonatal survival across the country, from all units.

Do premature babies born at these gestational ranges go on to have healthy lives?

The *EPIPAGE* study in France, which recently published its results, has shown that a large number of premature babies born below 26 weeks who survive go on to develop physical and learning difficulties with some requiring long-term support and care. This is true of babies in the UK too from the *EPICure* study of children born in 1995; these publications are widely available. In both countries, the rates of disabling conditions are much higher in babies of 23 weeks and below than at 24 or 25 weeks.

So why are some people still asking for the time limit to be lowered?

Some individuals and groups associate the lowering of the time limit with a lowering in the number of abortions carried out each year. Currently, only 2% of all abortions carried out in the UK each year occur between 20 weeks and 23 weeks and six days, and these are carried out in instances where the women's or baby's health are at risk. The vast majority of abortions occur within the first trimester of pregnancy Lowering the time limit will not result in a

the abortion time limit at 24 weeks allows women who find themselves in the above circumstances with recourse to act on an unwanted pregnancy.

What is the RCOG's position on the time limit of 24 weeks?

The RCOG believes that medical advancements have improved neonatal survival rates. However, there is currently a limit to successful interventions for premature babies which improve their survival rates. The abortion time limit should therefore stay at 24 weeks.

End notes and references

1. Costeloe K, Gibson AT, Marlow N, Wilkinson AR. The EPICure Study: Outcome to discharge from hospital for babies born at the threshold of viability. *Pediatrics* 2000 Oct; 106(4):659-71

2. Béatrice Larroque, Pierre-Yves Ancel, Stéphane Marret, Laetitia Marchand, Monique André, Catherine Arnaud, Véronique Pierrat, Jean-Christophe Rozé, Jean Messer, Gerard Thiriez, Antoine Burguet, Jean-Charles Picaud, Gérard Bréart, Monique Kaminski. Neurodevelopmental disabilities and special care of 5-year-old-children born before 33 weeks of gestation (the EPIPAGE study): a longitudinal cohort study; *The Lancet* 2008; 371:813-820

This briefing was produced in May 2008. Since this time the opinion of the Royal College of Obstetricians and Gynaecologists has not changed.

⇨ The above information is reprinted with kind permission from the Royal College of Obstetricians and Gynaecologists. Please visit www.rcog.org.uk for more information.

lower abortion rate. Women who are desperate to have an abortion will look for the means to have one, and this includes having an illegal and unsafe abortion in their own countries or travelling to a country where late abortions are carried out.

'There is currently a limit to successful interventions for premature babies which improve their survival rates. The abortion time limit should therefore stay at 24 weeks'

So what is the link between viability and abortion?

There is no link between viability with the calls for a lowering of the time limit, other than a very tenuous association. The issue of viability looks at the ability of babies to survive outside of the maternal womb. It examines the survival rate of premature babies. Medically, the longer the baby stays inside its mother (usually up to 40 weeks before birth), the better will be its outcomes. If a baby is born premature, doctors will do what they can to ensure its survival provided it is deemed to have a good chance.

The time limit on the other hand, is the cut-off point for abortions to take place. These are pregnancies which are unplanned and/or unwanted.

Apart from the argument about viability, why should the current time limit not be lowered?

There are many reasons why some women decide on a late abortion. The main ones are: an unplanned pregnancy, early pregnancy denial, late recognition of a pregnancy, a change in personal/financial circumstances, late referral to the abortion services, a late scan showing fetal abnormality. Keeping

Over half of women believe British abortion law is too permissive

Information from LIFE.

More than half of women in England, Wales and Scotland believe that the time limit for abortion should be reduced or that abortion should be banned in all cases except medical emergencies. A large-scale opinion survey by the polling company YouGov shows that women feel the current UK abortion law, which allows abortion up to 24 weeks of pregnancy for most reasons, is too permissive. 49% of women favour some kind of reduction in the time limit, with a further 5% favouring a ban on the procedure except in medical emergencies. Almost a quarter of all women (23%) believe that the abortion limit should be lowered below 20 weeks.

'37% of all those sampled – men and women – favoured some reduction in the time limit'

Women overwhelmingly reject any further liberalisation of the time limit, with just one in 20 believing that abortions for reasons other than medical emergency should be allowed after 24 weeks.

'Young people were significantly more likely to favour a reduction in the abortion time limit than older people'

More broadly, 37% of all those sampled – men and women – favoured some reduction in the time limit, with a further 6% favouring a total ban on abortion, meaning that at least 43% of people believe that the current abortion law is too permissive.

Young people (aged 18–24) were significantly more likely to favour a reduction in the abortion time limit than older people, with 43% favouring some kind of reduction. Another 8% of young people believe that abortion should be banned altogether, meaning that slightly more than half of 18–24–year–olds believe that the law as it stands is too permissive.

LIFE spokesperson Joanne Hill said:

'At LIFE, we have always recognised that significant numbers of people in the UK believe that our current abortion law is too permissive. These data clearly confirm that fact. In a week when the House of Commons is debating attitudes to sex education, we must think carefully about whether the abortion law is in touch with public attitudes.

'There have always been two arguments for the 24-week limit; that it represents a social/political compromise taking into account public opinion, and that it represents the lower limit of foetal viability. The second argument already looks weak in an age when the best special care baby units are regularly saving babies born prematurely before 24 weeks. Now the first is also looking shaky. It is time for policy makers to take note that the tide is turning against the liberal Abortion Act and take measures to respond to the expressions of concern from the public, especially women.'

⇨ Information from LIFE. Please visit www.lifecharity.org.uk for more information.

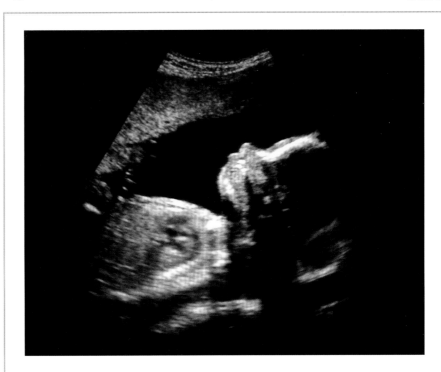

24 WEEK SCAN

Right to Know

The case for independent abortion counselling.

Overwhelming parliamentary support

⇨ A ComRes poll[1] has found that over 90% of MPs support the principle that women considering an abortion should have access to advice from someone who has no financial interest in the outcome of her decision.

⇨ 92% of MPs agreed with the statement that 'a woman should have the right to impartial advice when considering having an abortion, from a source that has no commercial interest in her decision'.

Private abortion providers and the NHS

The latest figures from the Department of Health[2] reveal the dramatic change in the role of private organisations in the provision of NHS-funded abortions over the past 20 years.

⇨ In 1991 the NHS funded 9,197 of the abortions carried out by the private sector.

By 2010 that figure had risen to 111,775 – an increase of over 100%.

⇨ In 1991 the NHS funded 10% of the abortions carried out by the private sector.

By 2010 that figure had risen to 93%.

⇨ In 1991 the NHS funded 84,369 abortions.

By 2010 that figure had more than doubled to 181,304.

The growth of privately-provided but publicly-funded abortions entirely accounted for this increase.

Private abortion providers' business practices

Private abortion providers have an incentive to increase the number of abortions that they perform, including those funded by the NHS. Both BPAS and MSI employ Business Development Managers, use commercial marketing techniques and promote abortion through advertising materials.

For example, achievements identified by BPAS over the past two years include:

⇨ An increase in procedures of 13% against a background of falling national trends.[3]

⇨ A key role in the development of [Department of Health] policy regarding the commission and provision of abortion services.[4]

⇨ BPAS' stated goals for 2011–12 include:[5]

⇨ Increase the number of NHS contracts by seeking expansion in the North East, East Midlands, South West and North London.

⇨ Generate a surplus of £2.2 million.

The urgent need for independent counselling

Lucy's story ...

One woman's story, reported in a recent Sunday newspaper article, provides just one example of why the provision of independent abortion counselling is needed.[6]

'Four weeks ago, Lucy had been due to give birth to her first child. But she never had her baby because last Christmas, Lucy chose instead to terminate her pregnancy. It is a decision that now haunts her. On July 24 – her baby's due date – Lucy went to her local park in the Home Counties and released a balloon in memory of the child she never had. She cries most days, her sadness greatest when she has time on her hands. "If I'm sitting at home with nothing to do, I get upset because I think I shouldn't be bored," says Lucy, 26, "I should be rushed off my feet because I should have a baby by now. I know now I should have kept the baby." Lucy, who is a receptionist, blames the abortion clinic for failing to give her proper guidance. 'You feel like you are on a conveyor belt', says Lucy. It was one she was unable to get off. Having discovered she was pregnant on 21 December by a boyfriend with whom she had just split up, she had an abortion 17 days later on 7 January'.

Extracted from The Pregnant Pause, Sunday Telegraph, Sunday 28 August 2011.

Undercover investigation ...

The experience of an undercover reporter for a national newspaper reveals the approach to counselling that can be taken by private abortion providers.[7]

'My first call was to Marie Stopes, a nationwide network of sexual health clinics that provide private and NHS abortions. They claim to allow women "access to comprehensive, impartial and non-judgemental information" and all counsellors are members of BACP. On the phone, the operator repeatedly tried to book me in for a medical assessment, the first step to getting an abortion – despite me stressing that I hadn't yet made up my mind. I felt bulldozed into starting the

---

1. ComRes surveyed a representative cross-section of 154 MPs between 9th March and 4th April 2011. Data were weighted to reflect the exact composition of the House of Commons. ComRes is a member of the British Polling Council and abides by its rules. Full tables at www.comres.co.uk

2. Department of Health statistics on abortions provided in England and Wales (residents only).

3. BPAS, Annual Report and Financial Statements, 31 March 2011.

4. BPAS, Annual Report and Financial Statements, 31 March 2010.

5. BPAS, Annual Report and Financial Statements, 31 March 2011.

6. Extracted from The Pregnant Pause, The Sunday Telegraph, Sunday 28th August 2011; full article available at:

www.telegraph.co.uk/health/8727344/The-pregnant-pause.html.

7. Extracted from Abortion Undercover, Daily Mail, Tuesday 30th August 2011; full article available at: http://www.dailymail.co.uk/femail/article-2031572/Abortion-Mail-writers-investigation-counselling-services-poses-disturbing-questions.html

termination process and had to insist on having counselling. In real life, a worried woman might have gone along with whatever she was told ... That counselling session took place the next day in Bloomsbury, central London. It cost £80 for just 30 minutes, but would have been free had I been referred by my GP. It quickly became apparent that my counsellor, Temi, was quite happy to influence my decisions. Her overwhelming advice was that I "must" tell my boyfriend, even though there is no legal requirement to do so ... Nevertheless, the message seemed very much to be that abortion was the best option. "It goes against our very nature to have an abortion," she said. "But we do things every day that go against our very nature." ... The session came to an abrupt end after 29 minutes and I left not knowing the medical or emotional side-effects of abortion. Keeping the baby was not seen as an option at all. I thanked my lucky stars that I wasn't scared and pregnant for real.'

Extracted from 'Abortion Undercover', Daily Mail, *30 August 2011.*

⇨ Information from Right to Know. Please visit www.righttoknow.org.uk for more information.

Why women need a modern abortion law and better services

Information from Abortion Rights.

Current law out of step with public opinion

Control over whether, when and how many children to have is crucial to control over every other aspect of a woman's life. An overwhelming three quarters of people in Britain support a woman's right to make her own abortion decision.

Current law gives doctors a veto over women's decisions

In Britain, abortion is not legally available at the request of the woman. After a woman has decided that she wants to end her pregnancy, she has to persuade two doctors to agree to her decision on the basis of restrictive legal criteria.

This requirement is not only paternalistic, but more damagingly, it allows the approximately one in ten doctors who are opposed to all abortion the opportunity to delay, obstruct or even veto women's decisions.

There is no legal requirement for doctors to declare their conscientious objection to abortion but professional guidelines require that they do refer a woman on to another doctor immediately. Abortion Rights hears from women who's anti-choice doctors, instead of declaring their objection and referring them on, have wrongly told them that they are too late, that they have lost their pregnancy test results, that they are not entitled to an NHS abortion, that abortion is murder or who have refused to refer them to another GP. This is unacceptable. It is time for a modern law – where women not doctors made the abortion decision, like every other medical procedure.

Rights for the women of Northern Ireland

The British abortion law was never extended to Northern Ireland and women there still don't have access to safe legal abortion.

With the developments in the peace process in Northern Ireland and the re-establishment of the institutions, it is time women there had their own rights to abortion.

Unacceptable delays in service provision

There is no law requiring the NHS to provide abortion services. Levels of funding for NHS service provision have increased over the past ten years, but waiting lists still vary across Britain resulting in a 'postcode lottery' of delays.

The Department of Health has set a target for delays of no longer than three weeks. No government figures are published on waiting times but

I have made my decision. A second opinion is not going to change that!

research conducted by the All Party Pro-choice and Sexual Health group showed that 27 per cent of Primary Care Trusts delayed women beyond three weeks.

In Abortion Rights' March 2007 opinion poll, 72 per cent said it was not acceptable for a woman who had been referred for an abortion to have to wait beyond three weeks for the procedure. It's time these delays ended.

⇨ The above information is reprinted with kind permission from Abortion Rights. Please visit www.abortionrights.org.uk for more information

The case for independent counselling

Information from the Right to Know campaign.

Next week the House of Commons will debate new proposals that mean that every woman considering a termination should receive an offer of independent counselling provided by someone with no vested financial interest in the outcome of her decision. Under these moves counselling will be non-compulsory and will not be an obstacle to women who have already made up their mind.

For those women who have made up their mind and who don't want to take up the offer of counselling, they will be able to proceed in exactly the same way that they are today.

But for the first time ever, an offer of independent counselling will be made to all women requesting a termination. After these proposals are adopted, no woman will ever say again, that she felt rail-roaded through the process, or that she was on a conveyor belt and that 'no-one ever stopped to ask me what I want', because every woman will be offered access to this very basic level of independent support.

So why are these measures needed?

Every year thousands of UK women will have an abortion, for some that experience makes no major impact and life carries on as normal. For others, it can have a significant and lasting effect that requires follow-up post-abortion counselling, treatment and in some cases therapy.

Organisations like the British Association of Counselling and Psychotherapy have been working in this space for years. As it is their counsellors who are most likely to see women after an abortion, it is little surprise that they too have recognised that there are big deficiencies in the availability of pre-abortion counselling. The article, *A Woman's Right to Choose Counselling*, published on BACP's site makes many important points, two are extracted below:

'Few patients "mourn" their appendix when it is removed. Many women who choose abortion still 'mourn' the lost possibilities of the life that will not be. Several years ago the privately funded Post Abortion Counselling Service was established in London to cope with these very problems. However, that leaves the rest of the nation and those who cannot pay.'

For these women, independent counselling will offer a space in which they have the option of fully thinking through their situation.

At the most basic level our abortion system should contain checks and balances to enable women to fully explore their situation in a space that is designated solely for them. Experience tells us that this space doesn't exist and the system as it has evolved over the years doesn't stand up to scrutiny.

The amendments will introduce equity into the system. Women who pay for abortions privately, can afford to pay for independent counselling wherever they choose, but a woman who is referred to an NHS outsourced organisation for an abortion, is restricted to accessing counselling through that organisation alone. A captured market for the abortion provider.

Abortion providers are conflicted

The experience of women who suffer trauma after an abortion is one example of evidence that demonstrates problems with the current system. The other type of evidence can be found from scrutinising how private providers operate and where their emphasis lies.

Abortion providers such as BPAS and Marie Stopes operate in a very business-like way. I'm sure they feel like they do a good job, but when you examine their operating ethos, their obsession like emphasis on promoting the abortion choice, it's very easy to see that they are in a very conflicted position. This doesn't do anyone any good, least of all women who are forced to access their services.

In our report *The Case for Independent Counselling* we explore these conflicts further.

The report demonstrates that abortion providers are motivated to increase their revenues and grow their market share. Like any business, they employ business development managers; BPAS state that they see a 13% growth in the number of abortions that they perform as a "significant achievement". If it's a success to increase abortions, the converse is equally true; it cannot under any circumstances be a success if the abortion numbers go down. Is an organisation with this clear level of motivation the right body to be providing counselling? Not only this, but women who are referred to BPAS or MSI are prevented from accessing any other form of NHS-funded counselling.

Counselling, information and advice should be delivered in a completely neutral environment. A kind of woman-centred bubble, that allows the woman facing the situation to explore fully her own feelings and emotions. That is what the amendments to the Health and Social Care Bill will deliver.

It's purely an optional facility, but it is one that is very much needed and which will deliver a better outcome for women. Some commentators have said that the provision of independent counselling actually bolsters choice for women as it's about ensuring that every woman who undergoes an abortion, has the right to fully explore whether that choice is right for her, without being influenced by those with a financial vested interest in the outcome of her decision. These very basic changes are long overdue.

29 August 2011

⇨ Information from Right to Know. Please visit www.righttoknow.org.uk for more information.

The abortion counselling consultation is a con – which is why I pulled out

With a fact-free campaign, Tory MPs are attempting to bring the worst of the US abortion debate to British politics.

By Diane Abbott

Just when you thought it was safe to go out, the right wing of the Conservative party have resurrected their fact-free campaign about abortion counselling.

It is important to stress that there are already full guidelines on abortion counselling from the British Medical Association and the Royal College of Obstetricians and Gynaecologists. The Royal College guidelines state: 'Women should have access to objective information and, if required, counselling and decision-making support about their pregnancy options'. Such counselling may include:

⇨ Implications counselling: aims to enable the person concerned to understand the implications of the proposed course of action for themselves and for their family.

⇨ Support counselling: aims to give emotional support in times of particular stress.

⇨ Therapeutic counselling: aims to help people with the consequences of their decision and to help them resolve problems which may arise as a result.

Furthermore the Department of Health inspects and regulates abortion clinics, and their inspections have never thrown up breaches of the guidelines. But, undeterred by the absence of evidence, the anti-abortion lobby has thrown itself into a campaign to promote the need for more abortion counselling. They spew out non-facts in support of a non-problem. But their campaign provides a handy vehicle to attack the motives of the doctors, nurses and clinics involved in providing abortions and to revisit what is fundamentally an anti-abortion case.

Nadine Dorries brought this issue to the floor of the House of Commons last year. Unsurprisingly, she was voted down. Opinion polls show that the majority of the public are against her.

So, most people imagined that the issue had gone away. But the Public Health Minister Anne Milton has been working behind the scenes to achieve a political 'fix' that would enable the Government to bring in the changes that the anti-abortionists desire without any more inconvenient parliamentary debate. The Government had already made it clear that it believed it could bring in the changes without legislation, by simply changing the regulations. And Milton thought she could get cover for this by setting up an all-party consultation group on abortion counselling and promoting a phony 'consultation'. The 'consultation' would, in theory, offer a range of options. But there was no doubt which option the Tory anti-abortionists preferred and which option they would ensure that the 'consultation" was flooded with support for.

I originally agreed to attend the group in good faith. Although I knew abortion counselling already existed, I was interested in seeing if it could be improved. In particular, I was concerned about a range of faith-based counselling services. I also thought it might be possible to look at offering better counselling over a range of issues like still-birth and infertility. But after a couple of meetings it became clear where the group was going and I have now withdrawn. Last night I had to debate the issue on television with Nadine Dorries. Nadine is Parliament's leading anti-abortion campaigner and she has made no secret of the fact that she sees the abortion counselling issue as a way of driving down the number of abortions.

True to form, Nadine was ready with a barrage of untrue assertions. She claimed that the abortion clinics are just in it for the money; that the majority of people who attended the MP 'consultation' meetings were pro-choice; that I had played no part in the meetings, even that I had slept through one. As she walked off the television set Nadine's high heels clacked triumphantly.

The trouble is that Nadine's performance is everything that is wrong with the social conservatives that are resurgent in the Conservative party. They rely on a smokescreen of emotion and personal attacks rather than evidence. And they are attempting to import the worst of the American debate on abortion and other 'values' issues into British politics. It is no coincidence that a group of Tory MPs (many of them the same people involved in the abortion counselling campaign) are reported to be preparing for a campaign to resist David Cameron's proposal to introduce gay marriage.

Women's lives are too important to be just pieces on a political chess board. And the coming 'consultation' is a con.

27 January 2012

⇨ The above article originally appeared in the Guardian. Please visit www.guardian.co.uk for further information on this and other subjects.

Women considering abortions should get independent counselling, say doctors

Women considering an abortion should have independent counselling, doctors have said.

The option of counselling should be available for all women, and not mandatory as some politicians have called for, the British Medical Association annual representatives meeting heard.

But the organisation providing the abortion should not also provide the counselling because of a 'subtle conflict of interest', it was argued.

Proposing the motion, Dr Mark Pickering, a member of the Christian Medical Fellowship, said: 'I am not talking about enforced counselling or an imposed cooling off period. Any counselling should be non-directive. This motion is about extending choice for women.'

Dr Jan Wise, speaking against the motion said the cost of counselling would add £40 to £100 and argued that Parliament had rejected calls for counselling to be separated from the organisation providing abortions.

Prof. Wendy Savage, who is a spokesman for Doctors for Women's Choice on Abortion also spoke against the motion saying doctors were capable of explaining the pros and cons of the procedure in the same way surgeons do with other operations.

Dr Tony Calland, chairman of the BMA ethics committee said the wording of the motion was unfortunate in that it referred to counselling that was independent of the abortion provider, because in most cases the NHS provided the abortion and it was not being argued that the NHS should not also provide counselling.

For that reason, although the motion was passed, it will not become official BMA policy.

Marie Stopes and the British Pregnancy Advisory Service, which both provide abortions, also counsel women beforehand.

In 2011, there were 189,931 abortions carried out for women who live in England and Wales, a slight increase on the previous year and almost eight per cent more than a decade ago.

Last year, Nadine Dorries tabled an amendment which would have stripped abortion providers of their role in counselling women. She argued that abortion providers had a vested interest in counselling women towards having a termination.

'It must be wrong that the abortion provider, who is paid to the tune of £60 million to carry out terminations, should also provide the counselling if a woman feels strong or brave enough to ask for it,' she said.

'If an organisation is paid that much for abortions, where is the incentive to reduce them?'

Although the amendment was rejected, Dorries declared she had 'won the war' after the health minister Anne Milton announced that the 'spirit' of her plans would be embodied in a consultation.

The Dorries' amendment would have stripped non-statutory abortion providers such as Marie Stopes and the British Pregnancy Advisory Service (BPAS) from offering counselling to women.

This was designed to provide greater opportunities for independent counsellors, some of whom are influenced by pro-life groups, to provide counselling. NHS abortion providers would still be free to offer counselling.

27 June 2012

⇨ The above information is reprinted with kind permission from *The Telegraph*. Please visit www. telegraph.co.uk.

Dear Sir

LETTER FOR PUBLICATION

The motion debated at the BMA's annual conference this week did not call for counselling to be separated from organisations providing abortion [Women considering abortions should get independent counselling, say, doctors, 28.6.12].

In fact, when the Chairman of the Medical Ethics Committee responded to this debate, he welcomed the fact that there was no criticism of existing counselling provision. The motion simply states that when a woman specifically wants to speak to someone who is separate from the abortion provider, for non-directive counselling, they should be able to access this.

This reflects the BMA's long-standing position on this issue.

Yours faithfully,

Dr Vivienne Nathanson

Director of Professional Activities

British Medical Association

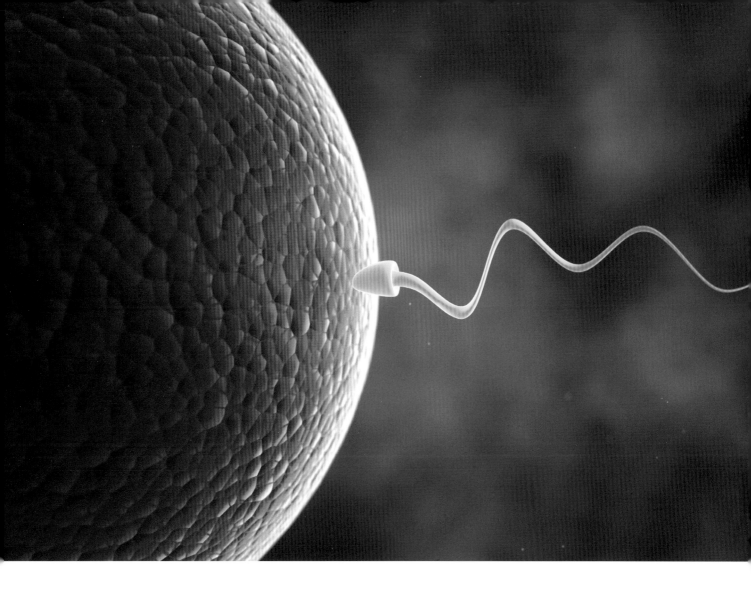

Non-directive abortion counselling wins backing

All women considering an abortion should have access to non-directive counselling, the meeting agreed.

However, doctors and medical students set aside a call for women to be able to access counselling that is independent of the abortion provider.

They noted the suggestion but stopped short of adopting it as policy. Yorkshire GP Mark Pickering said he had proposed the statement to increase choices for women considering terminations.

Dr Pickering said: 'I want to assure you this motion is not a pro-life stitch up ... For women who were certain that they wanted an abortion, this motion would not affect them.

'When I see women as a GP one of the most common phrases I hear is "I feel I have no choice" ... Every woman should simply know that if she wants to she can get counselling.'

Not independent of provider

But doctors and medical students were not convinced enough by the arguments that counselling for women should be independent of the abortion provider.

London consultant psychiatrist Jan Wise said the call was similar to a proposal by Mid Bedfordshire Conservative MP Nadine Dorries.

Ms Dorries tried to amend the Health and Social Care Bill to prevent services providing abortions also providing counselling. The amendment failed to make it into the legislation.

The BMA annual representative meeting also deplored 'picketing and intimidation' around abortion services.

27 June 2012

⇨ The above information is from the BMA. Please visit www. bma.org.uk

© BMA

Abortion investigation: doctor caught falsifying sex selection paperwork

A doctor who agreed to arrange an abortion for a woman wanting to end her pregnancy because her baby was a girl has compared it to 'female infanticide' while staff were also caught falsifying paperwork.

By Holly Watt, Claire Newell and Robert Winnett

The Calthorpe Clinic has been exposed for illicitly completing abortion forms amid concerns that doctors are not properly consulting patients before agreeing to terminations. A doctor at the clinic in Edgbaston, Birmingham, was also secretly filmed offering to arrange an abortion for a woman who said she wanted to terminate her pregnancy because the baby was a girl.

'All women seeking an abortion should have the opportunity to discuss at length and in detail with a professional their decision and the impact it may have'

'It's like female infanticide isn't it?' said Dr Raj Mohan before agreeing to conduct the procedure. So-called 'sex-selection' terminations are illegal.

Andrew Lansley, the Health Secretary, passed a dossier of alleged malpractice at the clinic to detectives. He also referred concerns over 'criminal' practices at two other abortion clinics to the police and General Medical Council.

The Daily Telegraph has this week exposed how abortion clinics

across the country are illegally offering to abort foetuses on the basis of gender. There are growing concerns about such practices taking place in Britain's abortion clinics.

It is understood that the NHS watchdog that monitors the clinics, the Care Quality Commission (CQC), had already alerted the Health Secretary to concerns over the documentation being used by the Calthorpe Clinic.

The head of CQC, which also oversees care homes and hospitals, resigned following a Department of Health report that criticised the quango.

The Telegraph carried out an investigation into sex-selection abortions after specific concerns were raised that the procedures were becoming increasingly common for cultural and social reasons.

In an article for this newspaper, Mr Lansley warns doctors that they will face the 'full force' of the law if they break the 1967 Abortion Act. 'Carrying out an abortion on the grounds of gender alone is in my view morally repugnant,' he writes.

'It is also illegal. Whatever an individual's opinion on abortion... laws in this country are decided by Parliament, not by individual doctors. If some professionals disagree with

the law as it stands they should argue their case for change. Simply flouting them in a belief that they know better is unacceptable.'

The Health Secretary added: 'Anyone indulging in illegal activity must understand that they are running a great risk. The potential penalty for breaking abortion legislation is imprisonment. Doctors could be struck off. And we will not hesitate to pursue any evidence which comes into our hands.'

Reporters, working undercover, accompanied pregnant women to nine abortion clinics around the country. Three offered to arrange terminations for women who said they wanted to end their pregnancy because they were unhappy with the sex of the baby.

When a woman who was 12 weeks pregnant had an appointment with a doctor at the Calthorpe Clinic, she explained that she wanted to terminate her pregnancy because she had discovered she was having a girl but her and her partner 'don't want a girl'.

'Is that the reason?' asked the doctor, who introduced himself as Dr Raj. 'That's not fair. It's like female infanticide isn't it?'

When the pregnant woman asked if he could put down a different reason for the termination, the doctor said:

'That's right, yeah, because it's not a good reason anytime ... I'll put too young for pregnancy, yeah?'

The patient agreed, at which point Dr Mohan again said: 'It's common in the Third World to have a female infanticide.'

He then moved on to discuss the abortion process before asking the pregnant patient to book an appointment for the termination the following Monday or Tuesday.

A nurse at the same clinic was also made aware that the reason for the abortion was because the patient 'did not want a girl' but did not object to the procedure taking place.

The patient was not offered any counselling and there was no discussion of the wisdom of her requesting the sex-selection abortion.

The disclosures are likely to lead to growing pressure for pregnant women considering an abortion to be offered independent counselling.

Mr Lansley says the Government will carry out a consultation on the issue and stresses that women should have the opportunity for detailed discussions with professionals.

'We will not only uphold that law, but it is why – in discussion with all main parties – we are planning to consult on counselling arrangements for women seeking an abortion,' he said.

'All women seeking an abortion should have the opportunity, if they so choose, to discuss at length and in detail with a professional their decision and the impact it may have.'

The Calthorpe Clinic, which declined to comment on the disclosures, is the third abortion provider to be exposed by The Daily Telegraph for offering gender-specific terminations. It is one of the country's oldest abortion clinics, having been set up in the late 1960s.

Yesterday's Telegraph disclosed how doctors working at Pall Mall Medical in Manchester and the Chelsea and Westminster Hospital in London were secretly recorded offering similarly illegal abortions, leading to widespread concern.

Dr Tony Falconer, president of the Royal College of Obstetrics and Gynaecology, said: 'Anecdotally, there are social and cultural reasons for preferring one gender over another and we need to know more about why these occur.

'The issues are complex. For instance, women may be coerced or threatened with violence into having an abortion. The priority would be to identify these women and to provide them with support.'

Anthony Ozimic, a spokesman for the Society for the Protection of Unborn Children, said: "This investigation confirms the reality of eugenics in modern British medicine, in which some innocent human beings are deemed too inconvenient to be allowed to live.

'Sex-selective abortion is an inevitable consequence of easy access to abortion, a situation to which the pro-abortion lobby has no convincing answer.'

However, Darinka Aleksic, the campaign coordinator of Abortion Rights, said the criminal practice of a minority should not be used to impose tighter restrictions.

'It is absolutely vital that abortion providers adhere stringently to both legal requirements and professional guidelines, so that the public has confidence in the system,' she said.

'But the fact is, abortion is heavily regulated and strictly licensed in this country.'

24 February 2012

⇨ Information from *The Telegraph*. Please visit www.telegraph. co.uk for further information.

Open letter of support for doctors who provide abortion services

Press release from Voice for Choice.

In the face of the *Daily Telegraph*'s attempt to entrap and discredit a number of doctors who provide abortions, we would like to express our support for all those doctors who are willing to provide abortion referrals in the UK and all health professionals who provide safe abortion services.

We represent pro-choice organisations that have been working for women's right to safe abortion for many years. We believe that abortion should be available to every woman who requests it, and that the provision of safe, accessible abortion care is a vital element of health care provision.

The Daily Telegraph's interpretation of the 1967 Abortion Act is mistaken. The law does not specify that rape is one of the legal grounds for abortion, but a doctor can provide a referral for abortion if a pregnancy results from rape. Similarly, abortion on grounds of sex selection is neither legal nor illegal in itself. Under the 1967 Abortion Act, it is the effect of the pregnancy on a woman's health, mental health and life that must be taken into account to determine whether or not she has grounds for abortion. Doctors are not given a shopping list of specific grounds for which abortion is allowed or not allowed. Rather, the law gives doctors the responsibility to decide whether the risk of continuing the pregnancy to the woman's health and mental health is greater than if the pregnancy were terminated.

In making this judgement, doctors are directed by the law to take into account the woman's personal circumstances. These include, for example, her age, her being unemployed or on low pay, or trying to complete her education, or being single, or having other small children to care for, or feeling strongly that she simply cannot cope with a baby (or another baby) at this particular time because of the negative impact it would have on her life, or because she has fears about the outcome and/or life chances of the child if it were born. The law further allows doctors to authorise an abortion if there is a risk to the woman's existing children of continuing the pregnancy, or if there is a risk of serious abnormality in the fetus if the pregnancy were to go to term.

The 1967 Abortion Act gave doctors the responsibility for authorising abortions in the belief that women could not be trusted to take this decision for themselves. Yet today, it is clear that women who have babies and women who have abortions are the same women. Today, most doctors and most people recognise that women themselves do know what is best for their own lives and do take responsible decisions. Hence, most doctors are willing to provide an abortion referral for a woman if she requests it because they understand that continuing an unwanted pregnancy is not good for women or their children, and will almost always cause a woman greater distress than having an abortion.

We believe the 1967 Act is outdated because it puts the onus on doctors to be gatekeepers, rather than providing women with the right to decide what is best for their own lives. We think that abortion should be available on a woman's request, and not be governed by criminal statute at all.

We are also opposed to gender discrimination, but sex selective abortion is not gender discrimination. Gender discrimination applies only to living people. A fetus does not have rights in the same way as a living person does, and therefore cannot be said to suffer from discrimination. Gender discrimination has its roots in economic, political, social and religious life; sex selective abortion may be one of the consequences of gender discrimination, but it is not a cause of gender discrimination.

The 'investigation' reported by the *Daily Telegraph* was carried out by unidentified persons in the context of concerted attempts by anti-abortion politicians and anti-abortion activists to discredit and frighten abortion providers by characterising them as unprofessional, greedy and wicked. Yet no evidence exists to support this proposition. Hence, they have stooped to using methods that are closer to entrapment than to any semblance of legitimate investigative journalism.

These methods are highly questionable if not downright unethical. In a video taken without the doctor's knowledge or consent, a short segment of which was screened on ITV's Granada Regional News on 23 February, a young doctor says to the bogus patient in front of her: 'If you want a termination, you want a termination. That's my job. That's all. I don't ask questions,' while the patient tries to insist on divulging her bogus reasons. This is not evidence of illegal behaviour on the doctor's part. That this doctor has since been suspended and the police asked to investigate her and others is a travesty of justice.

We would have hoped that pro-choice politicians would stand up for abortion providers, and maybe some still will. However, initial reactions have been hasty and heavy-handed, betraying underlying anti-abortion sentiments. Andrew Lansley, the Health Secretary, who otherwise claims he wants doctors to be in charge of all our health care services, said that doctors would face the 'full force' of the law if they break the 1967 Abortion Act. This is hard to swallow, especially considering that many of us hadn't even been born the last time a

doctor had to face the full force of the law in relation to illegal abortion. The Health Secretary should know better than most that the 1967 Abortion Act was formulated precisely to allow doctors to exercise their professional judgement. It is shocking that he would threaten them with prosecution for doing so on such flimsy evidence.

Some politicians, Nadine Dorries, for example, would dearly love to turn the clock back. She must be delighted that the *Daily Telegraph* has boosted her attempts as a woman to curtail other women's rights. In her blog on Conservative Home, she went one better than Andrew Lansley and threatened doctors not only with prosecution but with being struck off the medical register. She even mentioned life imprisonment, which is ludicrous, but intimidating nonetheless.

The vast majority of heterosexually active people of reproductive age are currently using a method of contraception to the best of their ability, but one in three women in Britain will have an abortion in her lifetime. We will stand up for doctors and other health professionals who support and are willing to provide safe abortion services. We applaud their commitment in the face of unwarranted harassment and condemnation. Even though the public are periodically showered with disinformation on abortion, every poll and every public debate show that most people in Britain are aware of and support the right to use contraception and the right of women to seek abortion when pregnancy is unwanted. We call on everyone who supports family planning, including safe abortion, to express their appreciation for the health professionals who provide them.

Signed by the following members of Voice for Choice:

Marge Berer, Editor, Reproductive Health Matters

Jane Fisher, Director, ARC (Antenatal Results and Choices)

Ann Furedi, Chief Executive, and Patricia A Lohr, Medical Director, BPAS

Lisa Hallgarten, consultant

Ann Henderson, Chair, Abortion Rights

Lesley Hoggart, Principal Research Fellow, University of Greenwich

Ellie Lee, Co-ordinator, Pro-Choice Forum

Wendy Savage, on behalf of Doctors for a Woman's Choice on Abortion

28 February 2012

⇨ The above information is reprinted with kind permission from the members of Voice for Choice. Please visit www.vfc. org.uk for more information.

© *Voice for Choice 2012*

Anti-abortion campaigners like 40 Days for Life have resorted to intimidation

Having lost the moral argument, the 40 Days for Life campaign has turned to bullying women out of their right to choose.

By Sarah Ditum

Something has changed in the UK's abortion debate. It's not that public attitudes have turned against choice – polling data consistently shows that roughly two-thirds of the population support a woman's right to terminate an unwanted pregnancy, with only a tiny proportion opposing abortion absolutely. But that tiny proportion has been extraordinarily successful in leading public and parliamentary discussion, and some have been alarmingly willing to adopt increasingly aggressive tactics aimed at abortion providers and the women they treat.

Outside the British Pregnancy Advisory Service's Bedford Square clinic in London, the anti-choice group 40 Days for Life has been holding what it describes as a 'prayer vigil'. For patients seeking the services of the clinic, and for those who work there, the effect of this gathering is undoubtedly one of intimidation. The women who attend there are already dealing with the anxiety of an unplanned pregnancy, as well as an imminent medical procedure and possible fears about how their family or friends might react to their choice. It's a moment when anyone is likely to feel vulnerable, and conscious of their privacy.

'Perhaps the anti-abortion movement has seen that it has lost the wider moral argument'

'We are very supportive of people's right to protest, but what we saw in Bedford Square was beyond the pale,' says Clare Murphy of BPAS. 'They hang around by the door and encircle women.' And 40 Days for Life's use of cameras is particularly disturbing. According to the organisation's leader Robert Colquhoun, photographic equipment is only used to protect the protesters, who he says have been threatened previously. But BPAS reports that the cameras have been turned on patients, in a tactic that amounts to harassment. Yesterday, 40 Days for Life tweeted to celebrate its first 'turnaround', but it's hard to imagine that any woman who has been repulsed by such intrusive actions is making a positive choice to be a mother.

Colquhoun stressed that all who attend the 40 Days for Life gatherings must sign a 'statement of peace' (available on the organisation's website), agreeing not to 'threaten, physically contact, or verbally abuse' staff or patients (inevitably, these are referred to as 'customers', using the same kind of 'abortion industry' language that Nadine Dorries has introduced to the House of Commons). However, he declined any suggestion that the statement could be rewritten to exclude filming, and as it stands anti-abortion campaigners may well feel that photographing women is a permissible non-violent activity.

At the weekend, another attack on the privacy of patients emerged, when a court heard how James Jeffery had hacked into BPAS's website, vandalised it and extracted database entries containing the details of women who had registered on the site. He told police he had been motivated by two friends having abortions he 'disagreed with'. Jeffery appears to have acted alone, and has no connection to 40 Days for Life; yet his extreme stance shows how much he has in common with the organised elements of the anti-choice movement. 'The letter he left on our website about the way abortion is "marketed" could have been lifted from a parliamentary discussion,' says Murphy.

'Cameras have been turned on patients, in a tactic that amounts to harassment'

The contemptuous attitude to women's privacy may feel familiar to those who have followed the debate about compulsory, medically unnecessary ultrasound scans for women seeking abortions in Virginia. When it was suggested that penetrating women with a vaginal probe might be a bit invasive, one proponent has suggested this wasn't problematic as the woman had already agreed to be penetrated when she got pregnant. In other words, to a certain anti-abortion mindset, to have had sex is to consent to any subsequent intrusion, whether that intrusion is of the body or of your private information. Perhaps the anti-abortion movement has seen that it has lost the wider moral argument and decided to try a different tactic: they don't need to convince the whole country, just intimidate enough individual women out of exercising their right to choose.

13 March 2012

⇨ This article first appeared in *The Observer*, 13 March 2012. Please visit www.guardian.co.uk for further information on this and other subjects.

40 Days for Life defends its methods against slurs

An interview with 40 Day for Life National Director David Bereit.

By Michael J. Miller

40 Days for Life is a grassroots movement to end abortion through prayer and fasting, constant vigil at places where preborn children are aborted, and community outreach to educate and mobilise the public. Nine coordinated national 40 Days for Life campaigns have been conducted since 2007.

Interviews with 40 Days for Life leaders David Bereit and Shawn Carney appeared in the January and February 2009 issues of *Catholic World Report*, as the movement was beginning to spread rapidly through the United States. *Catholic World Report* (CWR) recently contacted National Director David Bereit for clarifications about certain recent news reports.

CWR:

The 40 Days for Life campaign in London has been repeatedly accused in the press of 'bullying' or 'intimidating' women, even of pointing video cameras at women who go into the clinics. Participants in 40 Days for Life reply that they must sign a pledge to be non-confrontational. Are the vigils in London significantly different from the peaceful, prayerful demonstrations in the U.S.A.?

David Bereit:

The vigils in London use the exact same approach as those in the United States. Having just been to visit three of the 40 Days for Life campaigns in England a few weeks ago, including the London campaign, I can attest to their non-confrontational approach and to their use of the same statement of peace that we use.

Unfortunately a publication that regularly takes a 'pro-choice' position, *The Guardian*, simply regurgitated the abortion facility's false accusations without doing the research to find out that the cameraman in question was an independent person filming a documentary, who was not involved with 40 Days for Life. The 'bullying' and 'intimidating' actions they alleged were people praying, and others who were gently offering assistance to the pregnant mothers and referrals to local pregnancy help centres. The article was then circulated by other media outlets (including the Associated Press here in the U.S.A.) that did not even bother to check in with us or with the London 40 Days for Life leaders to verify or correct the accusations.

CWR:

Have the widely-publicised scandals involving Planned Parenthood changed the way in which the 40 Days for Life campaigns at those facilities are perceived?

Bereit:

The scandals at Planned Parenthood have significantly fuelled participation in 40 Days for Life campaigns held outside Planned Parenthood facilities, and we are seeing record numbers of people stand up against the abortion chain in communities coast to coast. We have also been encouraged to see two more Planned Parenthood abortion centres close during the current 40 Days for Life campaign, and numerous Planned Parenthood workers leave their jobs, thanking the 40 Days for Life participants who had been praying for them.

CWR:

Over the past two years the prospect of mandatory health insurance in the U.S.A. has politicised the debate over abortion even more. Has this in any way affected the ability of 40 Days for Life to plan and conduct vigils and to educate local communities?

> **'The scandals at Planned Parenthood have significantly fuelled participation in 40 Days for Life campaigns'**

Bereit:

If anything, the national debate about the abortion mandate in the Obama healthcare overhaul, and about the HHS mandate requiring religious employers to violate their consciences by paying for insurance with mandatory coverage of abortion-causing drugs, has awakened a sleeping giant. We are seeing record numbers of Christians getting active in pro-life efforts on every front. 40 Days for Life campaigns are growing larger than ever before, and we are seeing more positive results than in any of our past efforts. As people realise that the fundamental rights to life and religious freedom are under attack, they are finally coming out of their homes, workplaces and churches to take a peaceful stand for life and justice.

28 March 2012

⇨ The above information is reprinted with kind permission from *Catholic World Report*. Please visit their website www.catholicworldreport.com for further information on this and other subjects.

A day in the life of a pregnancy options counsellor

Cath Sutton, from BPAS London, talks through an average day in the life of a pregnancy options counsellor.

For the best part of 15 years I have worked as a counsellor for BPAS. Despite the length of time and the hours I've spent talking to the women I can confidently say there is only one constant, and that is that no day is ever the same.

Every single woman we see has a unique set of circumstances. She will feel a certain way about these and will require different things from the staff she sees during her visit.

Any woman with an unplanned pregnancy who comes to us will have a consultation. She will see a counsellor first, always alone, where we explore how she's feeling about the pregnancy, if she's made a decision and what support she has in place.

If she's clear that she wants to have the abortion, we make sure she is aware of all the procedure options and we can answer any non-medical questions she has about them. She will complete a medical assessment and then one of the counsellors can make her an appointment at the clinic.

If the woman is ambivalent, she has the opportunity to discuss her decision in more depth and from there .... well, there is no definite 'from there'. It could involve more time, more counselling, more information. Whatever the woman needs to make the best and most informed decision, we try and provide it.

It's hard for those who don't work in the clinic to understand how much support and understanding some women need. In the outside world everyone has an opinion about abortion, and it's generally expressed in emotive and judgemental ways. Even women who believe strongly in their right to

choose are often anxious that their reasons for having the abortion aren't good enough and that they will be punished for choosing to end the pregnancy at some point in the future.

There are no generic situations. We see women of all ages, of every colour and from every cultural and religious background. We can make no assumptions about any woman who sits before us in the counselling room. However a woman presents herself, or whatever her social background, there is no way of telling what she will need from us during her visit.

The most effective way of illustrating this is to talk you through a day. Yesterday, in fact. I arrive at work, I check the diary, catch up with my colleagues and then I call my first client from the waiting room. She is a woman in her thirties. She is clear about her decision – she and

her husband have two children, and they cannot afford a third. She is very sad though and is anxious about telling anyone, in case they don't fully understand their situation and judge her for being careless.

This woman cannot share all her sadness and anxieties with her husband, who is already worried about his job situation and is dealing with an elderly mother. But she can tell me; although the actual decision to end the pregnancy has been made we can talk about how she can look after herself – something she didn't feel she had the right to do.

My next client is a 17-year-old student, very clear that she wants the abortion. She is keen to complete her education and the idea of starting a family now is anathema. But she is very worried about whether to have a medical or surgical abortion – she needs

...WHATEVER YOU NEED TO FIND THE BEST WAY FORWARD...

me to describe in detail how the procedures work and what is involved.

Because we work in close conjunction with our clinics, I can tell this woman exactly what will happen from her arrival to discharge. I know that this has helped her, because she told me it had.

My third client is ambivalent. The pregnancy was planned, but as soon as she actually became pregnant her partner of over two years got cold feet and wants to end the relationship. She couldn't cope as a single parent but baulks at asking her parents for support, as they would find it difficult to accept her continuing the pregnancy outside marriage. They are deeply religious and they would, she thinks, be very disappointed in her if they realised what had happened.

This woman is a Christian herself and is struggling with the concept of abortion. She is trying to work out if she can reconcile her beliefs with her fear of being able to cope as a single parent and, simultaneously, the possible estrangement with her

family if she continued. We discuss adoption briefly but she knows this 'would kill her' – the idea of not caring for the child having gone through the pregnancy and birth – isn't one she can contemplate.

Many women feel the same about adoption or fostering – it would be too hard. But it would be wrong to dismiss this as an option, even if it only serves to concentrate the woman's focus on either abortion or becoming a parent. She decides in the end that she needs more time, so she leaves with our telephone number and the assurance she can return if she needs to talk more.

I then call through another very straightforward client – she is positive about her choice. She wants to travel and doesn't want to start a family, she is grateful there is somewhere she can have the abortion done safely. She is keen to talk about contraception, so the nurses and I do just that.

I then see a woman for post-abortion counselling. She had the procedure a week or so ago and is finding it difficult to cope. It becomes apparent that the relationship she was in had ended

and that she was in the process of re-evaluating her career when she found out she was pregnant. Although it was a hard decision, she felt that having the abortion was the right choice at the time, but she is now dealing with loss of the pregnancy, the loss of her partner, and the fear of staring a new job.

I spend the next hour or so booking women into the clinic for the procedure – I make sure they have all the relevant information and iron out any problems before they leave. One of the women I book is very tearful; she tells me she was so anxious and worried before she arrived but she feels everyone has treated her well and was friendly and helpful – something she wasn't expecting (or something she feels she didn't deserve, perhaps). Abortion care is not just about the woman's decision, it's also about her self-respect.

I want to emphasise that we are not saints – some days are difficult and frustrating, we can't always help women, and we cannot undo the series of events that have led them to BPAS in the first place. We cannot, in short, make the decision disappear and absolve them of this responsibility. But what we can do is see every woman as an individual and treat her accordingly. Listen to what she has to say and find the best way forward. We can give her the chance to talk to staff who believe that abortion is a choice.

It isn't enough for us to just provide her with the means to an end but to ensure that she doesn't feel demeaned by herself or others for choosing to have an abortion. On a good day, like yesterday, I feel I've gone some way to achieving this.

23 February 2012

⇨ Information from Abortion Review. Please visit www.abortionreview.org for further information.

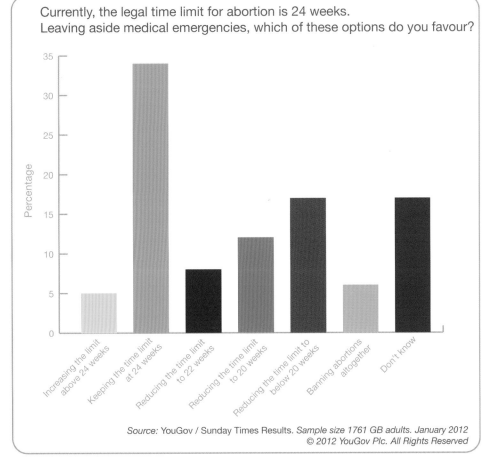

Currently, the legal time limit for abortion is 24 weeks.
Leaving aside medical emergencies, which of these options do you favour?

Percentage (y-axis: 0, 5, 10, 15, 20, 25, 30, 35)

Categories (x-axis): Increasing the limit above 24 weeks; Keeping the time limit at 24 weeks; Reducing the time limit to 22 weeks; Reducing the time limit to 20 weeks; Reducing the time limit to below 20 weeks; Banning abortions altogether; Don't know

Private abortion clinics free to advertise on TV

Private clinics offering abortions will be allowed to advertise on television under new regulations.

The Broadcast Committee of Advertising (BCAP) found 'no justification' to prevent commercial organisations offering a range of 'post-conception advice services' (PCAS) from engaging in TV advertising, providing they didn't use 'harmful or offensive' content.

Not-for-profit PCAS organisations are already free to advertise on television and radio.

According to the BCAP, the primary drive for the rule change was to ensure that advertisements for PCAS do not mislead 'potentially vulnerable' women in what services they offer.

'The new regulations will be enforced on public health grounds so that those women who do decide to seek a termination do not experience delays in obtaining

one, which would increase the risk of complications arising from the procedure,' said BCAS.

Under the new regulations, clinics offering advice on unplanned pregnancies must make it clear if the service does not refer women directly for a termination.

The new rules take effect on 30 April 2012.

Mark Bhagwandin, a spokesman for the Pro-life charity LIFE, said he is 'stunned' by the advertising watchdog's decision.

'It is easy to see: private abortion providers, made rich through the public purse, spending significant sums on advertising their product – abortion,' he said.

'It will represent a not unsurprising business model that has at its heart, the interest of money and

not of women. Where abortion businesses try to maximise profits through advertising their product, we are bound to see significant increases in the already extremely high number of abortions every year.

'The BCAP ruling is not in the interest of women and is deeply irresponsible.'

23 January 2012

⇨ The above information is reprinted with kind permission from Nursing in Practice. Please visit www.nursinginpractice. com for further information on this and other subjects.

© Nursing in Practice

Catholic midwives lose abortion 'conscientious objection' case

Information from the National Secular Society.

Two Catholic midwives have lost a legal battle after claiming that being asked to supervise nurses involved in abortion procedures violated their religious conscience.

The two women said being forced to supervise staff taking part in abortions at Southern General Hospital in Glasgow violated their human rights.

In judgement at the Court of Session in Edinburgh , Lady Smith said their right of conscientious objection was not unqualified and they had agreed to take up the roles of labour ward co-ordinators, although they now took objection to the job content. She added that 'They knowingly accepted that these duties were to be part of their job. They can be taken to have known that their professional body, the Royal College

of Nursing, takes the view that the right of conscientious objection is limited and extends only to active participation in the termination.'

NSS president Terry Sanderson said: 'These women knew when they started the job that the conscientious objection that is allowed only extends to direct participation in the abortion and not to supervising other nurses who might be working in that area. The court has made the right decision not to extend the scope of the conscientious objection otherwise where would it end? Would they be able to object to working in a hospital that carries out terminations? Or for a health authority that carries out terminations? They are perfectly entitled to their religious beliefs, but they must understand that not everyone shares them and if they don't want to do the duties that are

required of them, they should go into another line of work.

'Abortion is legal in this country and no woman undertakes it lightly. It is stressful enough without the added burden of dealing with disapproving midwives'.

This is the latest in a series of attempts by religious believers to put their beliefs above patient care. Like all previous attempts to secure special privileges at work, this one has failed.

29 February 2012

⇨ The above information is reprinted with kind permission from National Secular Society. Please visit www.secularism. org.uk/ for further information.

Key Facts

- In the 18th century, English common law allowed abortion, provided it was carried out before the mother felt the foetus move ('quickening'). (page 1)

- The Abortion Act of 1967 (as amended) regulates the modern process of abortion. The Act provides a number of criteria to be fulfilled before a pregnancy can be terminated. (page 1)

- The Offences Against the Person Act of 1861 made abortion a criminal offence punishable by imprisonment from three years to life. This was reversed by the Infant Life Preservation Act of 1929, which amended the law so that abortion would no longer be regarded as a criminal offence if it were proven to be carried out in 'good faith for the sole purpose of preserving the life of the mother'. (page 1)

- Abortion is not legal in Northern Ireland. The only legal reason for a woman being allowed an abortion is when there is a serious risk to her mental or physical health and the risk is permanent or long term. (page 3)

- One in three women admit to having an abortion by the age of 45. (page 4)

- There were 189,100 abortions in England and Wales in 2009, which is equivalent to 518 abortions being performed every day. (page 4)

- Abortion can be performed via two different procedures. Medical abortions are used from nine to twenty weeks of pregnancy and involve taking two different kinds of drugs. Alternatively a surgical abortion, which is performed after 15 weeks, involves a procedure called suction aspiration or dilation and evacuation. (page 6)

- In 2011, there were 189,931 abortions to women resident in England and Wales. This is roughly the same (a rise of 0.2%) from 2010. (page 10)

- In 2011 the age-standardised abortion rate was 17.5 per 1,000 women residents aged 15-44, the same as in 2009 and 2010. (page 10)

- To date, the highest rate for the number of abortions was in 2007, of 18.6 per 1000 women residents aged 15–44. (page 11)

- In 2010 the Total Fertility Rate (TFR) for England and Wales increased to 2.00 children per woman from 1.96 in 2009. There were 723,165 live births, compared with 706,248 in 2009 (a rise of 2.4%). (page 11)

- In 2010 about 60% of conceptions to women under 16 ended in abortion, as did about 12% of conceptions to women aged 30-34. (page 11)

- Statistics show that 26% of women who have abortions have had 'one or more' previous abortion. The proportion of women who have had more than one previous abortion is roughly 9%. (page 11)

- Research shows that women who have more than one abortion are no less likely to use contraception, and are certainly not using abortion as a means of contraception. (page 12)

- In England and Wales abortion is widely available. The proportion of abortions funded by the National Health Service has risen steadily, and in 2011 96% of abortions were funded by the NHS, compared to 94% in 2009. (page 12)

- Research conducted by Priscilla Coleman suggests that women who undergo abortion face nearly double the risk of mental health difficulties compared with others and that one in ten of all mental health problems was a result of an abortion. (page 14)

- No religion actively supports abortion but some religions accept that there are situations when abortion may be necessary. A few religions oppose abortion under all circumstances. (page 19)

- The legal limit for most abortions was reduced from 28 weeks to 24 weeks in 1990 because some babies now survive at 24 weeks. (page 20)

- Just one in 20 women believe that abortions for reasons other than medical emergency should be allowed after 24 weeks. (page 23)

- Three quarters of people in Britain support a woman's right to make her own abortion decision. (page 25)

- In Britain abortion is not legally available at the request of the woman. After a woman has decided that she wants to end her pregnancy, she has to persuade two doctors to agree to her decision on the basis of restrictive legal criteria. (page 25)

Abnormality

An abnormal or disformed feature. With unborn babies or foetus's this can refer to a disability or feature which would prevent a child from leading a relatively normal and happy life once it was born, and can, therefore, be a reason to terminate a pregnancy.

Abortion

A procedure which prematurely ends a pregnancy through the death and expulsion of the foetus. It can occur naturally (spontaneous abortion), but this is more commonly referred to as a miscarriage. The term 'abortion' usually refers the deliberate termination of an unwanted pregnancy (induced abortion).

Conception

The act of fertilisation, where an egg (ovum) joins together with a sperm (spermatozoon) to form an embryo or zygote. This term describes the moment a woman becomes pregnant.

Contraception

Anything which prevents conception, or pregnancy, from taking place. 'Barrier methods', such as condoms, work by stopping sperm from reaching an egg during intercourse and are also effective in preventing sexually transmitted infections (STI's). Hormonal methods such as the contraceptive pill change the way a woman's body works to prevent an egg from being fertilised. Emergency contraception, commonly known as the 'morning-after-pill', is used after unprotected sex to prevent a fertilised egg from becoming implanted in the womb.

Embryo (zygote)

Between day 14 and week eight of pregnancy the fertilised egg is referred to as an embryo. A zygote is simply the scientific term for the fertilised egg which is made by the joining of an egg (ovum) and sperm (spermatozoon). After the eighth week of pregnancy an unborn baby is referred to as a foetus.

Female infanticide

Infanticide is the unlawful killing of very young children and babies. Female infanticide specifically refers to the practice of killing female babies and young girls and is a practice that has been reported in India, China and parts of Africa, Asia and the Middle East.

Gestation

The development period of an embryo or foetus between conception and birth. As the exact date of conception in humans can be difficult to identify it is usually dated from the beginning of a woman's previous menstrual period.

Neonatal

Referring to an unborn child, or the period of time before a child is born.

Obstetricians and gynaecologists

An Obstetrician or Gynaecologist is a person who specialises in treating diseases of the female reproductive organs.

Paternalistic

Referring to the act or practice of managing other individuals.

Pro-choice

Pro-choice supporters believe that it is a woman's right to choose whether or not to continue with a pregnancy. They also believe that the choice to have an abortion should be available to all.

Pro-life

Pro-life supporters believe that life begins at the moment of conception and think that an unborn child, foetus or embryo has the same rights as any other living person. They believe that the law should be changed so that abortion would be heavily restricted or outlawed in the UK.

Terminate

A term meaning 'to bring something to an end', an abortion is sometimes referred to as a termination.

The Abortion Act 1967

This act decriminalised abortion in cases where it had been certified by two doctors that certain grounds had been met, such as a serious risk to the mental or physical health of the pregnant woman.

Viability

This refers to a foetus's ability to survive outside the womb. In UK law, the 24th week of pregnancy is the point at which the foetus is considered to be viable, and therefore the latest point at which an abortion can be performed. However, some people have argued that this should be reduced as medical advances mean that some premature babies born at 24 weeks, or fewer, are surviving.

Assignments

The following tasks aim to help you think through the debate surrounding abortion and provide a better understanding of the topic:

1. Research Deng Jiyuan and his wife Feng Jianme and the 'forced abortion case' in China that was reported in the spring and summer of 2012. You may want to look at several newspaper websites, including *The Telegraph*, and BBC News for their coverage of the case. Use this research as a discussion point in your class to consider how it might provoke responses from Pro-life and Pro-choice campaigners. What ethical, political and medical issues do you think this case raises?

2. The Abortion Act of 1967 (as amended) regulates the modern process of abortion. The Act provides a number of criteria to be fulfilled before a pregnancy can be terminated. Do you agree with these criteria? Do you think that other criteria should be added to the list?

3. Looking at 'Chapter 1: Terminating a pregnancy', create a leaflet that will inform young people about the abortion procedure. In the leaflet you will need to explain the facts about the medical procedures involved, along with the emotional side-effects and the moral issues related to abortion.

4. 'Some people categorise abortion as murder at even the earliest stages of pregnancy.' (page 18) Do you agree?

5. Create a poster displaying the different religious views surrounding abortion, you may find the article on religion and abortion in Chapter 2 helpful (page 19).

6. Imagine you are a pregnancy options counsellor. A young woman who is eight weeks pregnant has come to see you; she is unsure about whether she wants to continue with her pregnancy. Using the information presented throughout this book, create a bulleted list which provides your patient with a collection of unbiased options and advice surrounding abortion and its alternatives.

7. Hold a debate in your class with one half of the pupils representing the views held by Pro-life campaigners and the other half representing those of Pro-choice campaigners. For information you should refer to the articles provided in 'Chapter 3: Abortion debate in the media'.

8. Research the historical attitudes surrounding abortion since the eighteenth century. How has public perception, the legality of abortion and women's ability to determine whether they keep their pregnancy or have an abortion changed over time? Record your findings in a timeline which shows these gradual historical changes. For information you might find Chapter 1 of this book helpful along with the BBC's website: http://www.bbc.co.uk/ethics/abortion/legal/history_1.html

9. Conduct a survey asking your classmates whether they are for or against abortion, and whether they would consider themselves as Pro-life or Pro-choice. Draw conclusions from your survey and consider the following: How does your class' feedback match up to the information provided in the *Statistics briefing 2012* and *Abortion* sections found in Chapter 1 of this book?

10. Visit www.lifecharity.org.uk and www.spuc.org.uk/education/charities and research these organisations. Working in a group consider how the information these websites provide might affect the choices of a young woman who finds herself unexpectedly pregnant and considering the option of a termination? You may also want to consider how Pro-life and Pro-choice campaigners might interact with these organisations? Present your findings in a PowerPoint presentation to your class.

11. Write an article which will explore the following question: 'Why is it important to educate students about contraception, pregnancy and abortion?'

12. Visit www.bbc.co.uk and research recent news articles which discuss issues surrounding abortion. How do the news items relate to the articles and data presented in this textbook?

13. Conduct online research about global perceptions on abortion. Draw up a table which compares and contrasts these findings with UK attitudes. To start with, you may find the article *Abortion investigation: doctor caught falsifying sex selection paperwork* in Chapter 3 helpful (page 30).

14. Watch the film *Vera Drake*. Write a review explaining whether you think the film is Pro-abortion, Pro-life or Pro-choice? What other messages do you think the film portrays to its audience, and what does the film say about the consequences of abortion?

Acknowledgements

The publisher is grateful for permission to reproduce the following material.

While every care has been taken to trace and acknowledge copyright, the publisher tenders its apology for any accidental infringement or where copyright has proved untraceable. The publisher would be pleased to come to a suitable arrangement in any such case with the rightful owner.

Chapter One: Terminating a pregnancy

Abortion, © 2004–2012 SquareDigital Media Ltd, *Abortion laws*, © Brook, *Abortion: the full story*, © Charlotte Fantelli, *Abortion: what happens*, © Department of Health 2011, *Alternatives to abortion*, © UK Health Centre 2012, *Men and abortion*, © 2011 Lighthouse Family Trust, *What the statistics tell us*, © Abortion Review, *Abortion increases risk of mental health problems, new research finds*, © Telegraph Media Group Limited 2012, *Systematic review of induced abortion and women's mental health published*, © Academy of Royal Medical Colleges.

Chapter Two: Ethics and abortion

Abortion controversy: pro-choice and pro-life, © UK Health Centre, *Moral and ethical issues*, © Education for Choice, *Religion and abortion*, © Education for Choice, *Disability and abortion*, © Education for Choice, *The abortion time limit and why it should remain at 24 weeks*, © Royal College of Obstetricians Gynaecologists, *Over half of women believe British abortion law is too permissive*, © LIFE, *Right to Know*, © Right to Know, *Why women need a modern abortion law and better services*, © Abortion Rights, *The case of independent counselling*, © Right to Know, *The abortion counselling consultation is a con – which is why I pulled out*, © Guardian News & Media Ltd 2012, *Women considering abortions should get independent counselling, say doctors*, © Telegraph Media Group Limited 2012, *Non-directive abortion counselling wins backing*, © BMA.

Chapter Three: Abortion debate in the media

Abortion investigation: doctor caught falsifying sex selection paperwork, © Telegraph Media Group Limited 2012, *Open letter of support for doctors who provide abortion services*, © Voice for Choice 2012, *Anti-abortion campaigners like 40 Days for Life have resorted to intimidation*, © Guardian News & Media Ltd 2012, *40 Days for Life defends its methods against slurs*, © Catholic World Report, *A day in the life of a pregnancy options counsellor*, © Abortion Review, *Private abortion clinics free to advertise on TV*, © Nursing in Practice, *Catholic midwives lose abortion 'conscientious objection' case*, © National Secular Society.

Illustrations:

Pages 3 and 9: Don Hatcher; pages 8 and 25: Angelo Madrid; pages 31 and 36: Simon Kneebone.

Images:

Cover, pages iii and 29: © Jezperklauzen; page 6: © Kurhan; page 17: © Anna Levinzon; page 22: © woewchikyury; page 23: © mathieukor; page 33: © Sean Locke; page 38: © jian wan; page 39: © notoryczna.

Additional acknowledgements:

Editorial on behalf of Independence Educational Publishers by Cara Acred.

With thanks to the Independence team: Mary Chapman, Sandra Dennis, Christina Hughes, Jackie Staines, Jan Sunderland and Amy Watson.

Cara Acred

Cambridge

September, 2012